Full Circle

Margery Bloomfield

with letters from Odd Irtun

Also by Margery Bloomfield

TREE OF LIFE

A history of the European School of Osteopathy –
and much more…

Matador
9 Priory Business Park
Kibworth Beauchamp
Leicestershire LE8 0RX, UK
Tel: (+44) 116 279 2299
Fax: (+44) 116 279 2277
Email: books@troubador.co.uk
Web: www.troubador.co.uk/matador

ISBN 978 1784620 417

British Library Cataloguing in Publication Data.
A catalogue record for this book is available from the British Library.

Cover design by Matt Drew

Printed and bound in the UK by TJ International, Padstow, Cornwall

Matador is an imprint of Troubador Publishing Ltd

www.margerybloomfield.co.uk

For Odd – as promised

Chapter 1

The Arctic Circle, March 2010

I decided to go up on deck away from the pointless chatter. I needed to think.

It was breathtakingly beautiful – white-crested waves rolling by, snow-covered mountains sparkling in the distance, the dull throb of the ship's heart as we snaked our way down the coast of Norway. Fairly soon the sun would be going to bed but before its final embrace with the horizon, it was sending a ballet of colour pirouetting across the sky; shocking pink melting into shades of coral, peach and apricot ending in an explosion of brightest gold illuminating the puffy clouds. It was magical, otherworldly, even a little mystical. I felt my eyes fill with tears. Beauty often has that affect on me.

In the pocket of my Arctic jacket, my hand still clutched the slip of paper I had been given in Narvik. Was I going to make that telephone call, or not? Perhaps the past should be left undisturbed, beautiful, distant memories allowed to slumber on through all eternity.

I pondered various possibilities, what if his wife (if he had one) answered the phone? Of course, it occurred to me that he could be dead; it was some 55 years since we parted. Perhaps he had had a son who bore his name and this was the son's telephone number in my pocket. Then again he could be alive still but ill in hospital, or away on holiday, or perhaps when I rang he would be out somewhere. Questions, questions – all unanswerable.

With the passage of time I had thought of him less and less of course, but I had never forgotten him. Never. I guess the first big, meaningful love has a way of leaving its print on one's life forever. The burning question was, had he forgotten me? Half a century plus is a very long time! The worst scenario would be if I made the call and he only vaguely remembered me – or perhaps not at all! How deflating that would be. Another ghastly thought sprang to mind, he might have developed dementia.

What age would he be now? He was older than me for sure, but how much – two or three years – or four – or more? I knew his birthday was the August 18th, but which year? Such details have no importance when one is in one's early twenties – and madly in love.

More hypothetical questions ran riot through my head. What if ... what if...?

Enough!

Of course I would make the phone call – there was never any doubt. Everything else apart, my curiosity would win the day.

How would I announce myself? He would not know my married name and he never called me Margery, always Marge.

I returned to my cabin and, without further ado, I dialled the number. Three rings – and it was answered. I recognised his voice immediately and felt a bit panicky. What do I say? What do I say? My opening gambit was unusual to say the least.

"Are you about 80 – and is your name Odd?" I asked in English. A pause then slowly, also in English, he replied, "Y-e-s."

"Do you remember a young Australian girl you met in 1951…" I had not even finished the sentence before he exclaimed, "Marge, Marge, *my* Marge, is that really you?"

"Yes, it is," I replied, "and is that really Odd?" We both laughed.

"Where are you?" he asked.

"At sea," I answered.

"Which sea?"

"I am on a cruise ship sailing down the coast of Norway and due to arrive in Trondheim tomorrow."

"You, Marge, here in Trondheim tomorrow – unbelievable! Oh, we must meet." Yes, indeed.

As we talked, all those years without any contact at all suddenly melted away like snow in the sun. This was turn-back-the-clock time and it felt as if nothing had changed, we were still 'connected'. Our conversation flowed with the same relaxed, easy intimacy that we had always shared. There was so much to ask and tell each other.

One of the first things he said was that he had always had a guilty conscience about me because he knew he had caused me suffering.

"Life is what happens when you are planning other things,"

I said. After a thoughtful pause I added "Anyway, that was all a long time ago."

He was curious to learn how I had found him. "It's an amazing story. One of our ports of call on the cruise was Narvik and I had booked to go on a shore excursion in the morning. We went by cable car up the mountain. The snow was deep, the sunshine brilliant and the blue sky cloudless. As I stood there drinking in the beauty of the scene, I thought of you, Odd. As Narvik was where you had spent your youth, suddenly I had a mental picture of you skiing down the slopes that were right there in front of me. I could not but help wonder what your life had been like.

Later in the day, cosily encased in my Arctic jacket and snowboots, I was walking around the town when I came to the Tourist Information Office and a spontaneous idea flashed through my mind. I went in and asked if they had a telephone directory. "Sorry, no." I was about to leave when the girl said, "Who are you looking for; perhaps we can do something to help?" I explained that I had known a man – over half a century ago – who had been born and brought up in Narvik and on an impulse I had wondered whether there might be some trace of him or perhaps a member of his family. I added that I did not expect my enquiry would yield a result. By this time, I had reached the door and was about to leave when she said, "Let me try the Internet for you."

In minutes, she said, "There is somebody by that name. As a matter of fact, he is rather well known in Norway – a writer, a poet actually. Could that possibly be your friend?"

"Yes," I replied. "Without any doubt." Then she added, "Oh, what a shame, he doesn't live here anymore." "I understood her to mean that you didn't live in Norway anymore which did not surprise me at all. I recalled that you were multi-lingual and well, you could be living anywhere in the world." "No," she continued, "I'm afraid he lives now in Trondheim."

"Trondheim, Trondheim," I gasped. "That is where I am going tomorrow!" How serendipitous, I said to myself.

"I reflected that I had been to Norway a number of times since we parted but it had never occurred to me to try and contact you. After all, the past is the past. You can't put the toothpaste back in the tube!" I joked. "It was just being in Narvik that had sparked my spontaneous action."

We chatted on for some minutes – then came something I did not want to hear.

"How are you in health, Marge?"

"Very well, thank you, and full of energy as ever – and you?" I enquired.

"I am coming to the end of my life, I'm afraid. I have inoperable stomach cancer."

I was stunned and overwhelmed with sadness. "But things are not too bad at the moment," he continued, "and, of course, I will come to the ship tomorrow." We agreed to meet at 3:00 p.m. and I would wait at the gangway.

"Will we recognise each other?" he asked.

"Yes," I said, "we are the same people, just older – a lot older – and, hopefully, wiser."

As we would have only a couple of hours together, I wondered whether there would be anywhere close by where we could sit and talk. I decided the best thing was to request permission for

Odd to come on board. It was *not* granted. With all the terrorist precautions these days, I was told that 72 hours' notice was required. I explained the situation and, eventually, I was asked to complete a form which would be 'considered' but it was doubtful that my request would be granted.

During the latter part of the cruise, I had met up with three couples with whom I had enjoyed some amusing evenings. I had agreed to have a drink with them before dinner. I told them what had happened to me that day and they loved the story.

One of the wives, returning later to the bar, said she had seen the Captain and told him it was really important that permission be granted. Sure enough, the following morning, I was told that all was well, he could come on board.

I had a feeling he might be early so I stood at the top of the gangway just after 2.30 p.m. Very soon, a taxi pulled up, quite some distance from the ship and I knew it was him. There were tentative waves from each of us which quickly became vigorous. I beckoned him to come up on board – and, well, we just fell into each other's arms. How incredible it was to meet again after such an eternity. He asked immediately if I was with anyone (he had overlooked checking on that small point when we spoke on the phone). "No," I said. "I am travelling alone." We went straight to my cabin. At first, we just sat, clasped hands and looked at each other in sheer disbelief. Was this really happening?

Odd then delved into the bag he had brought with him and produced a number of pages from a photograph album. There were our images from 1951 when, with my Mother, I had gone on a tour of Scandinavia and met Odd who was the Tour Manager, a summer job he did during the years of his university studies. There were quite a number of group photos as well, and we noticed that somehow we were always side-by-side. Photographs too from Holland and some taken later in London. We were so bright-eyed and full of smiles, the way one is when love is in the air.

The next thing Odd produced from his bag was his most recent book of poems which he had written whilst recovering from the first lot of cancer treatment. He told me that when he was given the 'bad news' he could just have waited to die – or he could have written another book of poems, this time about facing death and reviewing his life. He decided on the latter course of action and the poems were very favourably received. He showed me many press reviews all of which highly acclaimed his most recent book. He even found the courage when he was discharged from hospital to give a poetry reading in a local church.

I then told Odd that I too had written a book and I had a copy with me as I had planned to offer it to the ship's library but had not yet done so. He was clearly delighted to hear that I had also taken up my pen. My book was a history of the European School of Osteopathy, which I had co-founded with my first husband.

We then wrote messages in our respective books and exchanged copies. From my book, Odd would discover much of what my working life had been about during the intervening half century.

Out of the blue, he said suddenly, "Wouldn't it be funny if we ended up together?" Indeed it would, I mused. Then he added, "It wouldn't have worked before, would it?"

"Possibly not," I replied, "but we'll never know!"

Even more unexpected was, "I remember every inch of your

body – show me your feet!" As I do not care for crazy whist, bridge or carpet bowls, I spent some hours whilst at sea in the beauty salon to pass the time. As luck would have it, I had had a luxury pedicure the day before so was quite happy to kick off my shoes and flaunt my bright red painted toenails and smooth-as-satin skin – at his command!

How utterly crazy, I thought to myself. We have only been together for some 25 minutes, after total silence for 55 years, and he is sitting here in my cabin massaging my foot! Mind you, if he had said show me your breasts, I would have acceded with the same alacrity to his request, such was the feeling of instant and natural togetherness, an immediate connection that was beyond words. We were behaving – and feeling – as if we were in our twenties again, the same playfulness and humour that always ran alongside the deeper feelings.

"Push up your sleeve" he said. I obeyed and he turned my arm over and ran his index finger very gently along the inside of my arm. I took a deep shuddering breath. He smiled with satisfaction. "I am so glad you are still responsive to my touch." I returned the smile and said "And I am glad you haven't forgotten how to make my pulse race."

I was unashamedly flirting with him and he was flirting back. How amusing I thought to myself. A pair of 80 year olds still doing what they always did so well. And why not?

I learnt that his wife, Sigrid, had died suddenly in 2001 whilst they were holidaying in Cyprus and I told him that I had lost my Robert in 2004 from vascular dementia. I had nursed him for seven long and heartbreaking years. He had been my second husband.

The first marriage had been successful – until it wasn't, 14 years later. We divorced but went on working together, which was not a particularly easy thing to do but essential for the continuance of the school we had founded.

As we talked, it became clear that our lives had followed somewhat similar pathways. On the whole, we had both had happy marriages and successful, satisfying careers, both having been Heads of Schools. Neither of us had had children with our main partners although Odd had a daughter from a marriage way back in the mists of time. I had had two stepdaughters from my first marriage and five stepchildren from my marriage to Robert. Philosophically, I had been drawn to the East, in particular to Buddhism, and Odd also had some leanings in that direction. We chattered on, finding so many things in common.

Before long, the topic turned to sex which had played quite an important part in our relationship when we were in our twenties – and rightly so! We reminisced about some of the highlights, some of our creative moments and some of the funny ones too. "…That incident in the Rose Court Hotel when the manager all but kicked us out, telling you not to bring whores to his establishment. With great dignity you said, 'How dare you, this lovely lady is the woman I love and hope to marry.' Of course, in retrospect, we could see how he got the wrong idea. We arrived at midday – without any baggage – and booked out again about 4.30 p.m. the same day! And remember that spaghetti dinner in my bed-sit? The things one can do with spaghetti!"

Then Odd said, "We would have been in bed by now."

"Very likely," I replied.

"Shall we?" he asked. I hated to be practical at this delicious moment in time but I reminded him that very soon he would have to leave the ship. He shrugged his shoulders with a resigned but impish grin on his face. "I think we invented sex, Marge."

After exchanging addresses and telephone numbers, we made our way to the gangway. Odd said to the officer on duty, "How much do you think the Captain would accept as a bribe to stay here another night?"

"Probably more than you have, Sir," came the reply. Odd asked me not to wait until he had disappeared but to go back into the warmth of the ship.

I sat in an armchair close to the gangway looking, I am sure, somewhat dazed. A woman I had spoken to several times during the cruise came up to me and asked, "Are you alright, dear?"

"Yes," I replied.

"Are you sure? You don't look alright," she insisted. I then found myself telling her, in brief outline only, what had just happened. When I finished, I looked up at her and she had tears rolling down her cheeks and her lips were trembling. "That is the most romantic story I have ever heard. It has made my trip," she sobbed.

As she disappeared down the stairs to her cabin, probably to have a good cry, she turned and said, "Oh, you *must* see each other again. You must!" Silently, I agreed with her.

That evening, as arranged, I met up with the three couples with whom I had become friendly – Anne and John, Pam and Pete, Jenny and John. They were most interested to hear how the meeting had gone. It appeared that quite a number of other people on the cruise had also 'taken an interest' – news travels fast on a cruise ship! Various people I had never even spoken to came up and said, "We saw your friend coming up the gangway," or "going down the gangway," or "we saw you saying goodbye." What was going on – why all this interest? I guess it's just that everyone loves a love story.

Later, after dinner, back in the bar, Anne passed me her mobile and said, "Do feel free to ring him to say goodnight." I accepted gladly and Odd sounded very pleased to receive my call. He told me he could still feel my hands in his. Incredibly, I had exactly the same sensation. As we said goodnight, he added, "I am so pleased you found me."

That night I couldn't sleep. The excitement of the day had me in a spin. I threw on some warm clothes and went up on deck to commune with the stars. When the cold night air became too much I returned to my cabin and wrote him a letter – although I never posted it.

At Sea

My dear special Odd,

Just a few hours ago we were sitting here in my cabin holding hands. Was it a dream?

Seeing you again, Odd, after such a long, long time was a beautiful confirmation of life itself. I am so glad you exist.

The ease and speed with which I found you was amazing. From that spontaneous thought in Narvik, it took only *minutes* and I had your telephone number. Equally amazing, my next port of call was Trondheim.

How easy was that!

The years melted away so quickly as we talked – AND with the same intimacy as those two 20-something year-olds. Proof – if one needed it – that when a bond has been really strong, it stands the test of time – and whatever else life throws at it.

With you in thoughts

Your Marge

Chapter 2

I arrived back in the UK on April 2nd, Good Friday. That evening, we spoke at length on the telephone. Odd was due to leave for France on the Sunday to spend some weeks in the sun visiting friends, in the hope that it would help restore some measure of health after such a bleak winter in Norway, the worst in decades, plus his long spell in hospital and all the side-effects of chemotherapy.

By the time he got back from France, I was in Morocco visiting my dear friends Paloma (Picasso's daughter) and her husband Eric – and what a wonderful stay I had with them!

It was May therefore before I heard from Odd again – and then there were lots of long telephone conversations covering a myriad of subjects. For example:

"I remember the clothes you used to wear, Marge. You had a style all your own and you always looked so chic."

"It wouldn't have worked back then would it?" He had said that before and I did wonder whether he was still trying to deal with his guilty conscience. My answer was the same, "Possibly not, but we'll never know."

"Are you rich, Marge?"

"No, are you?"

"No, I'm not either. However, I have no complaints about my situation. It's fine."

Then I added, "At various periods of my life, I have been rich-ish, poor-ish and everything in between. Right now, I would say I have enough to do what I want to do. Some people call that 'comfortably poor'."

"When you visited the UK in 1960, Odd – which was five years after we parted – *why* did you contact me?" There was a long silence and then he said, "Why not?" There were lots of things I could have said in reply, but didn't. He added, "It was a very brief meeting, wasn't it?"

"Yes, no more than half an hour, as I recall. It was quite a shock when you rang me to say you were in London and could we meet for a drink. I had only been married to Tom a couple of months but, against my better judgement, I agreed. We were to meet two days hence and, during that interval, Tom became ill with 'man flu' – psychosomatic no doubt, as I had told him previously about our relationship and he probably viewed our meeting again as some kind of threat. He took to his bed coughing and moaning, which was a lightly veiled hint that I should not leave him. I explained that I had to lay a ghost to rest; I promised I wouldn't be long. Do you remember that meeting, Odd?"

"Only vaguely."

"I'm rather vague about it too, except for two memories.

One was how awkward it felt seeing you again. My heart was pounding and I felt I had to keep my distance from you, not even a handshake. The other thing I remember was removing my glove and showing you my wedding ring. The rest is a blur. When I got home, I told Tom I never felt a thing. Did I lie? The speed with which he recovered from his illness was astonishing!"

And then we exchanged letters.

In his first long letter dated May 13th 2010, Odd told me of his reactions to our meeting again. Referring to my first telephone call from the ship, he wrote:

I recognised you at once, the tone and the hidden laughter in your voice, as if you had not been away from my life all these years … how was it possible that this could happen? Was there a thick cable through the waves of the North Sea with secret signals that I was going to meet you, you never forgotten, Marge, with the sweet flavour of our twenties.

I have sometimes wondered how it would be to meet a certain someone from the crossroads – who had printed their sign in my heart and my memory.

Was it going to happen now – and a sudden mixture of reactions filled me – surprise, pleasure, dreams and – elements of reality. Was it possible? Somewhere in the clouds I flew and flew and the idea was strengthened. Was I going to meet you again, see you, feel your nearness? It flashed through me. It was difficult to control oneself.

But you were there, standing at the top of the gangway. It was raining, it was cold, but I felt excited, happy like a child having his birthday. These moments are so rare. I recognised you at first sight. It was you, Marge, and you hadn't changed a bit, the smile was there, your eyes, the sound of your laughter. How strange to meet again. Was it real?

The words came back as if they had never stopped. We were the same in a way, the openness, the nearness, the spontaneity of feelings nourished by the memories from the 1950s.

Yes, I felt awakened! Time went so quickly. In the evening the telephone rang – "I had to say goodnight, Odd." How sweet, how right, how you. How homely like!

I have a feeling that we feel very much the same way. This was life's reward to both of us. Both tied together with this wonderful spontaneous impulsiveness, looking for a garden of roses on our evening walk.

After two days, I have discovered that the eye of reality has kept looking at me as if asking: who is the most (or least) *realistic* of you two? A very unpleasant question indeed – and I answer quickly – when happiness in the form of a lovely woman invites you, say *yes* please! But the unpleasant eye insists. Remember the possible difficulties. And here we go. I told you I was sick. Half a year ago I met the gravity of my situation at St Olav's Hospital in Trondheim. The diagnosis was 'Incurable Cancer in the stomach. Nothing to gain by an operation'.

I took it in a quiet way.

In the months that followed, I wrote another book (the one I gave you on the ship), mainly poetry: the meeting of death and memories from a life story. The reception was good in the press and all this was probably good medicine. I began to feel better, encouraged by the hospital staff, lovely women. No pain, no vomiting and a gradual lifting of the spirit. Then I decided to go to France, to Antibes, where I have friends and where I had stayed many times.

It helped to make me feel better. Long walks and French food got me in better shape. I had reduced my weight by 21 kilos. And now, after one week at home, I still feel OK, or even better. On May 20th, I have a hospital control of the situation. So far they cannot say anything about the length of my life but I don't think so much about death, and all my friends encourage me a lot and say I begin to look like I did before.

But there is another thing. In Antibes, I stayed with Marie, a 'girl' of my age I met in 1945. We were more than friends.

In 1958, when I married Sigrid, Marie was so depressed that she left Norway for France – Paris, 10 years. Antibes, 30 years. She worked for two famous artists, painters, and lived a very interesting and exciting life, meeting all the top people, from Presidents and you name it. It sounds as if you and Marie had a similar life, participation in something great. I did not see her for 40 years.

The trouble is that after Sigrid's death, it seems she still loves me very much, but I cannot return her feelings. She is a good and loyal friend, and an unusual woman. She is not jealous but broad-minded and generous.

I have told her about you and our rendezvous in Trondheim, as indeed I have told all my friends (they think it is a wonderful story).

But if you and I get together (!) … the time I have left … what will happen to her? Long before this – between you and me – she said a wise thing to me. "Remember, Odd, you are not responsible for me. If I feel depressed and unhappy for some reason, it is up to me to build myself up." I admire her for that and many other good things.

Maybe I go too far now in my expectations for our relationship. I probably do. Maybe to meet you, to talk and enjoy each other's company (oh, God) will be what life has to offer us at this stage. We have to take one step or one day at a time, as the saying goes. (But the problem is that I am still only 25!).

Before I let you react to these lines in my letter, I must add that I was impressed by your book, a life's work, seriously engaged, an intellectual achievement. I enjoyed the style of writing. You have kept your spontaneous impulsiveness. Also, then that I am proud of you! I did not know the sources of seriousness in your character at that time. We were too innocent and immature. You have impressed me!

I am counting the days till I get your answer!

Your awakened Odd

And I replied:

May 19th 2010

My dear Awakened One!

Your letter has just arrived. It was worth waiting for – and as I read your thoughts and reflections, my pulse quickens. The thing that amazes me is the similarity of our responses to this – what shall we call it – 'incredible happening'. As you want a quick response from me, I have just telephoned – but there is no reply. Perhaps you will ring me back when you get my message.

Meantime, I am going to have some lunch in the garden. It is such a spectacularly beautiful day here – wall-to-wall sunshine and clear blue skies. The garden is now lush, very green with a riot of colours from the Spring flowers, some with a haunting fragrance. The birds are singing their hearts out and my two ponds are teeming with life. As if that is not enough, I have a nesting pheasant! With any luck, I shall have some little pheasant chicks wobbling around the garden in a day or two. On top of all that beauty, I have found you again! A-maz-ing…

Back indoors now – and we have just spoken on the phone. Yes, of course, we *must* meet again.

This 'incredible happening' as I've called it almost felt as if it had been orchestrated by some 'independent force'. I don't know how else to express it. Perhaps I am being too mystical but, yes, it does feel as if we have been given a precious gift. When one thinks about it, it must be extremely rare for two people to meet again, after total silence for over 50 years, and *instantly* feel so connected – no small talk, no polite preliminary chit chat, just an immediate closeness – which clearly we both felt.

The prospect of revisiting our relationship with that wonderful openness that we both value – and its attendant sense of 'freedom' – really excites and fascinates me. I am looking forward so much to our journey of discovery!

It is quite like old times to be writing to each other again. We did such a lot of that half a century ago. Somewhere I am sure I still have some of your letters. When I married Tom, I thought I should destroy them. After all, the past was well and truly relegated to the past. You had married somebody else, I had married somebody else. We would never meet again – but in the wings of life's stage the Voice of Destiny chuckled, "We'll see about that!" Who was it who said never say never?

When it came to destroying your letters, I found I just could not do it. You had been an important part of my life and I reasoned that burning your letters would not erase that. Instead – and I remember this so vividly – I tied them up in a bundle, put the bundle in a large plastic bag and sealed it with a whole reel of Sellotape wound round and around. What on earth was I trying to do – keep you in or keep myself out? It seems more likely that I was trying to discourage anyone who, one day, might be tempted to pry. The bundle screamed 'Private – Keep Out'. Anyway, I must locate those letters as I think they could make very interesting reading – for both of us!

I mentioned on the phone that I had looked out some old photographs of us from way back – some taken in

Norway, others in my Kensington bed-sit, and a few in Hyde Park. You asked me to send them – but they are mainly of you, so I want to keep them, please. However you might like the one of us (enclosed) in a fond embrace taken, as I recall, with the camera's self-timer. It occurs to me that what could be interesting for you – if I can find them – would be photographs taken every 10 years (there were always decade-busting birthday photos) so you can see how your Marge has changed/developed/aged over the last 50 years. You so sweetly insisted that I hadn't changed a bit (and there's nothing wrong with a white lie!). However, if you find that the smile and the laughter in my voice are the same, that'll do. We know we are the same people and that's all that matters.

It is now the May 21st, gone midnight and I'm feeling sleepy, so will sign off until tomorrow.

Thank you so much for telling me about Marie – but I knew! Well, not that it was Marie of course, but I was certain that you had gone to France to stay with a woman friend (rather than 'friends'). I guess they call it female intuition – and I have it in abundance. Actually, back in the early 50s, you told me all about your special friendship with Marie. In fact, I think I met her very briefly. You were in London on travel business and I was with you. Then Marie arrived in London and she sent you one – no two – red roses.

Does that ring a bell? I have a very hazy memory of a young girl (weren't we all then!) of medium height, an athletic build and brown hair. Does that sound anything like Marie in 1950 something? As I say that part of the memory is hazy but the red roses I remember well. In a way it confirms what you told me then – and now. Obviously she has always been in love with you but, as you say, you have never been able to return her feelings in spite of your – equally obvious – great fondness for her. Chemistry is inexplicable, isn't it? If it exists between two people it absolutely cannot be denied. But if the chemistry does not exist, one cannot invent it, nor fake it. That's the story of love I guess.

I smiled when I read that you have been telling all your friends about our meeting again – and they think it is a wonderful story. I have done exactly the same and, yes, *everyone* thinks it is a wonderful story – and I agree with them! It is interesting too how touched people are by it.

So, when-where-how do we meet again? I think we know why (two hours, after all those long years, was not enough). But I agree totally, we must take it one step at a time … where and how? Norway, as you suggest, is fine with me. Is there an airport at Trondheim?

When? How about the June 18th? The details I leave entirely to you. Let me know your thoughts – soon!

Your impatient Marge

By the next telephone call, we had settled on the date. There was a direct flight to Trondheim on June 17th – and I was booked on it! In the days that followed, Odd was full of ideas in our daily phone chats about what we could do – take a steamer up the coast of Norway to the Lofoten Islands and rent a fisherman's cottage, or take the car to the Sylane mountains near the Swedish border and stay overnight with the cuckoos wishing us welcome, or go touring in the car, or ... I stopped him in mid-sentence. "Odd," I said, "I am not coming to Norway to go sight-seeing, as lovely as all your suggestions sound. I am coming to see *you*!"

A few days later, I received another letter from him, dated May 30th 2010.

My dearest Marge

The other night when I was sitting indulging in my thoughts of you coming here, I recalled something a friend of mine had said. "How long will she stay?" In my imagination I hadn't given space for such unpleasant things. When I asked you on the telephone, you said what is probably the 'sensible' thing (I hate to admit that) – "Two weeks for a start."

Then another thing – where to stay? "With me, of course," I had said. But on reflection, I feel it might be an idea for us to stay in a nice hotel for the first couple of nights. Is that OK with you?

The activities we shall enjoy, we can discuss when you get here. One step at a time, wasn't that what we agreed upon?

I must admit that my volume of energy is not as big as it used to be. What I enjoy more and more are the quiet things but, of course, mixed with social activities and Nature. Don't worry, I will be open for all your wishes!

I look forward immensely to having you here – as my sunshine – to talk about all the things I want to hear about your life … just to be near you, near you, do you hear? My dear Marge, how strange after all these years. I remember the pleasant heartbeat and the scent of your body.

The apple tree is blooming against my window. The garden is big and green now, not yet ripe but more like a virgin.

I am so happy that you found me.

Your Odd

For the following 10 days before my departure, it was difficult to think of anything, other than my visit to Odd, this special man from the frozen north who, all those long years ago, lit a flame in my heart that was never totally extinguished.

Was I nervous about the visit? No, the two hours we spent together on the ship, the long daily phone calls since and the letters … everything had felt so natural. Of course, there had not been a man in my life since Robert's illness and death, so I guess I should have felt, at the very least, a little apprehensive – but I didn't!

I hunted high and low for Odd's love letters which I was certain I still had. Then just the day before I was due to depart, I had a mental image of the bundle in the bottom of the old pine chest in my study. Sure enough, the curious package was there, smiling up at me in a knowing way as if to say, "I am a long dormant volcano about to erupt again!" I cut off all the Sellotape and took the letters out of the plastic bag. The contents smelt musty with age. I had forgotten the letters were wrapped as well in one of his handkerchiefs which he had signed and added "*Jeg elsker deg*" (I love you) – and I had embroidered the words in red silk thread. When

I set out on my year-long round-the-world travels (an incredible 21st birthday gift from my Mother), I took with me a large white scarf, with the idea that if I met interesting or famous people along the way, I would ask them to autograph the scarf. However, when I met Odd, I knew he was far too special to sign the general scarf – hence his own signed handkerchief.

I sat up all night reading the letters – so many of them – as well as loving messages written on restaurant brochures, cards, hotel receipts, paper serviettes and scraps of paper. I seemed to have kept everything! There was also a silver bracelet with a Viking ship charm and a locket containing his photograph, as well as a small-framed photo of him, which had been on my bedside table during most of my twenties. Then, of course, there were all the letters he wrote to me when I was back in Australia for 15 months, before returning to Europe for good – but they got left behind in Melbourne. Reading those beautiful love letters was such a strange experience, as if I was eavesdropping at the door of life or, put another way, I felt almost like a 'voyeur' of my past, our past!

It was difficult to take it all in, so many memories that I had buried, indeed that I had to bury in order to get on with my life. However, I was so glad that I had not destroyed those lyrical love letters. If only Odd had kept mine, which he didn't (perhaps it is more of a girl thing), then this book could almost have written itself.

Chapter 3

I was up at silly o'clock to get myself ready and now here I was at the airport about to embark on my Nordic journey of rediscovery. I felt incredibly lively and excited, a bit like a Duracell bunny! I decided to make a maximum purchase at the Duty Free Shop of the drinks we had most favoured in our wild youth – gin, red wine, champagne – and cigarettes for Odd, as he told me he had given up in his 40s (just as I had) but had started again when he became ill. A feeling of 'what the hell', I guess. I took my purchases to the till and was unfortunate in being served by a truculent young woman who was also unbelievably slow. The last call for my flight was announced. I grabbed the goods and ran as if being chased by wild bears; of course it *would* be the most distant gate. I was the last passenger to board the plane. How really awful it would have been if I had missed it!

For the duration of the flight, I let my mind wander across the years. We had been born at the opposite ends of the earth but when we met our heartstrings very quickly became entwined. Now, after 55 years of not being in each other's lives, we were going to be together again. Doesn't life play the most extraordinary games! That gossamer thread that once bound us together had proved to be indestructible, no matter how many years had passed. It was rather like one of those birthday candles that you can't blow out. The flame may die down but it is never completely extinguished.

My thoughts strayed back to Odd's letter of last month, his first one to me after meeting again. He was saying how much he had enjoyed my book "*Tree of Life*" adding, "I didn't know the sources of seriousness in your character at that time. *We were too innocent and immature*, you have impressed me!" Well, for sure, *I* was innocent and immature when we first met – a 21-year-old virgin who had led a rather sheltered life in Australia. Odd was four years older but, to me, he seemed so worldly and experienced. Of course, I had had my share of teenage romances – and at 21, two proposals of marriage – but he was the first man who had captured my heart and my imagination. I suppose our totally different backgrounds were part of the attraction but, above all, it was a 'connection' so strong that it defied any kind of label, a deep understanding without words. Such an experience stays in your blood – forever.

Memories of my youth in Australia then began to wash over me. I had a very happy, secure childhood, loving parents, an adorable sister eight years older who named me, so I was told, three years before I was born! When travelling on public transport she would say to my Mother, 'We must leave a space for Margery'. I guess she really wanted a little sister.

The air hostess brought my gin and tonic and I sank back into another reverie. These two weeks that we were about to enjoy would be the longest period of time *in one go* that we had ever spent together. How incredible I thought to myself. In the 50s we snatched 'us time' whenever and wherever we could – a few days, a weekend, a night, a week max. There was always so much separation, in fact come to think of it, probably some 80% of our relationship happened through our letters, which were so full of longing. Of course, when we did get together it was sheer magic, so in the moment, so rapturous – but then, we were in our twenties. What would it be like now I wondered – well, I would find out soon enough. The Captain announced that we would be landing in Trondheim in 10 minutes.

He was there waiting for me, all smiles and big hugs. Just before leaving, Odd had rung me to say, rather than drive his own car to the airport, he had asked his friend, Arne Jørgen, to take him to collect me and then drive us both to the hotel he had booked for the first couple of nights. This arrangement, he explained, would allow us to sit in the back seat and hold hands straight away! Clearly, he had thought of everything – well, nearly … when we booked in, we found that our charming room had twin beds. He had booked a double room but forgot to specify a double bed. "What the hell," he grinned, "we'll push them together."

After unpacking, Odd poured us a drink and then, much as we had done on board the cruise ship, we just sat, clasped hands and looked at each other, still with disbelief that this was actually happening. The world felt strangely still and quiet, a world-stop-turning moment, I guess, as if we were frozen in time. So many questions hung in the air, where to start?

In no time, we seemed to slide seamlessly into our old relationship, we were back in our twenties and I felt so grateful that we had both been blessed with the youth gene! In a recent letter Odd had told me he was only 25 and I told him I owned up to being 36 – permanently. In fact, my 80th birthday celebrations (which had lasted for a solid week due to my wonderful friends) had included a 1920s party, which I hosted. The invitations clearly stated that it was my 36th birthday party. On the back, there was a photograph of me as a baby and another at 36 – and the words read from 0 to 36 – in 80 years. We were in complete agreement that age is all in the mind and, that being so, it was equally joyous to discover that the body concurred!

It was time for bed – surely this was one of life's OMG occasions. Our bodies tangled. I had to hold back the tears. There were no words that could express the sheer intensity of feelings. After a lifetime apart, we were together again, entwined and clinging.

Then, at absolutely the wrong moment, the twin beds drifted apart and Odd disappeared down the crack onto the floor, with a bang! I roared with laughter – and so did he, eventually, after he picked himself up and climbed back into bed. Why is it that some of the most romantic moments of my life have also been some of the funniest – but then humour can be very sexy.

The next couple of days it never stopped raining, but we were more than happy to stay put in our hotel – and mainly in our room with the 'Do Not Disturb' sign hanging on the door (we didn't give a damn what the hotel staff might think).

After two days, it was time to pack up and go to Odd's flat.

What an interesting apartment. The walls were covered with paintings, many by famous Norwegian artists who were friends, plus drawings, photographs (some of me, I noticed) and books, books and more books. It was warm and cosy but it was obviously the home of a smoker, and ever since I had given up in my 40s, I found a smoky atmosphere quite difficult to cope with. I did not want anything to upset this special time so made a decision there and then. Odd was making a coffee so when we sat down at the kitchen table, I asked him to light two cigarettes. If you can't beat 'em, join 'em! I vividly remembered how much we had enjoyed smoking together (in the days when everyone smoked) and, rather romantically, he always lit my cigarette for me. As we were now turning back the clock, why not include smoking. Problem solved! I then indulged in that Norwegian habit (or was it an Odd habit?) of putting a sugar lump in my mouth and drinking the coffee through it. Delicious!

"I seem to remember that you always drank black coffee, Marge."

"Yes, I did, for many years, which brings to mind an amusing little story. Back in the early 1950s, London 'discovered' Italian coffee and coffee bars sprang up all over the place. My particular favourite was in Knightsbridge, I went in there one day on my own, found a nice corner table and began to read my book. A waiter approached and said "And what would you like?" With my head still in my book I said "A large black please" and when I looked up, he was! At least 6'4. Fortunately he had a sense of humour, clicked his heels, gave a little bow and said "At your service." We both went off into peels of laughter."

The first puff of a cigarette felt strange.

"What age were you, Marge, when you started smoking?"

"14. I had gone on a hike with some friends and we were being attacked by mosquitoes in a wood. One of the young boys said that cigarette smoke would soon get rid of them. Nobody smoked so we decided to make our own out of dried pine needles we gathered, then rubbed together until they became powdery. The 'powder' was then rolled into pieces of newspaper to form cigarettes – and we all lit up. It was revolting – and we had sore throats for days – but it did reduce the mosquito attacks.

I was 17 before I tried again. I was soon hooked and continued until my 40s when, finally, after many failed attempts to abandon it, it gave me up by way of a chest infection that turned into pneumonia.

I was living with Robert by this time and he too was a life-long smoker. He decided he was being unfair continuing to smoke when I had stopped. Typically he chose a dramatic course of action. He told me he was going to 'disappear' for a weekend. He moved into the spare room with a jug of water and locked himself in – no food, nothing to drink but water, no conversation or human contact of any kind. On Monday morning he emerged, threw away his remaining cigarettes – and never smoked again. I was so proud of him.

It was time to read some of those letters, now in chronological order so that they could reveal our story. Odd asked me to read them aloud.

The day I was leaving Australia in 1953, I received two airletters from Odd which I put in my handbag and took with me. The rest were left behind in Australia (I wonder what happened to them?).

Narvik, March 26th 1953
Dearest Marge

Thank you for your lovely letter which I have read many times. The time is approaching very quickly ... when we shall meet again. I hope it will be realised ... how are your plans going?

I wonder how you are at present. Marge – my dream – my necessary dream in a grey reality. How beautiful isn't it? I have a warm secret whenever I look at your photograph. And just this vague unknown background is part of the attraction.

You said you are willing to face reality. That is good. Personally I have had too much of it lately. So much that I want to forget it. I do not want to go into details.

Narvik April 14th. I have found this letter which was not finished before my holidays this Easter, so why not send it? I wrote you an airletter yesterday with information about my arrival in London in June. And I have also received your wonderful message about your coming to England in the immediate future.

I am in an awfully bad mood at present, depressed, and I only look forward to get away from here. South to the sun and the vitality.

What do you think our meeting will be like? I can hardly wait, Marge.

Narvik, April 11th 1953

Dearest Marge

It sounds wonderful. 'You are coming'. It is not to be believed. And it is only a little airletter that conveys that striking information. At the beginning of June we should be able to meet. Imagine that, dear Marge.

As you can see I am still here in Narvik. I have just returned from a fortnight in the mountains with sun and snow. And now it is more teaching and scientific work. I am sorry I could not answer your two beautiful airletters before now. They are always a sensation and they bring *you* to my heart.

There is so much I want to write about but there is no time. I hope I'll reach you with this before you leave Australia.

What is left unsaid here, we will take up when the Great Moment brings us together.

Your Odd

The next letter reached me after my arrival in the UK. It was from Paris dated May 28th 1953.

"...you are in London. And I am here. I cannot yet realize what it means. You know Marge we have been calculating in years – and now you are here. Frankly speaking it has been a dream – and now it is reality and I wonder, just like you, what sort of reality we are facing...

What are the words that can express the interlude before

our meeting again? It is like that moment immediately before a concert fills the waiting audience.

I won't be back in London with my party of 25 South Africans until July 9th which is a long time to wait. I suppose there is no chance of seeing each other before then?"

I looked at Odd and asked him if he remembered our incredible meeting again after nearly two years of writing to each other. "I don't remember everything," he admitted, "but I know I had that bad news to tell you and you were wonderful about it. How many days did we have together then, four or five maybe, but we packed a lot in and I particularly remember our heartbreakingly sad goodbye when that taxi took you away from me."

Thinking back to 1951, we recalled that actually we had very little time together. There was the Scandinavian Tour when we first met, which lasted about two and a half weeks. Although our mutual attraction had been building gradually during that time, we didn't really get together until towards the end. "In particular," Odd interjected, "on the ship crossing the North Sea. I remember that well. I thought you knew what you were doing when you agreed to come to my cabin for a nightcap but then you told me you were a virgin. We made such sweet love that night but I respected your wishes and you remained a virgin."

"Your understanding and sensitivity really impressed me. Some men might well have taken advantage, but you didn't. And there was something you said that night which has stayed in my memory. You picked up your toothbrush from the basin next to the bed and you said "The essence of a really happy marriage is when the couple use the same toothbrush."

"Did I say that? How very unhygienic of me" Odd chuckled.

"Be that as it may" I replied "it was the bigger meaning of what you said that grabbed me, and that is why your words have lingered over the years."

After the Tour, there were only two or three other meetings, all rather short. "I remember vividly the first one. I was in Scotland with my Mother. You arrived in London with a few days free before starting another Tour. You rang me and asked if I could join you. Mother's reaction was a touch histrionic. Clearly she had realised there was something quite serious going on between us and I guess she was terrified of her daughter becoming involved with a Norwegian – and all that might mean. Rather to my surprise, she feigned a heart attack in an attempt to stop me from going to London. It was obviously an act and I didn't buy it, so off I dashed to meet you."

"You remember so much detail, Marge," Odd said. "I realised you had that facility of course from reading your book."

"Yes, I have been blessed with a very good memory – and I can certainly recall exactly what it was like when we met again in 1953, with all its joy – and its sadness. Above all else, the magic was still there, the chemistry, that incredible connection – whatever one calls it, it was still there in abundance." Of course nearly two years had gone by during which we had both had all sorts of experiences and relationships. I told Odd that I had met a Russian in 1952. He was nearly twice my age, an interesting man whose company I thoroughly enjoyed. I went out with him for nearly a year. Odd had already guessed what came next… "and you are no longer a virgin?"

"Correct," I said.

"I can't hide the fact that I am really sorry the privilege was not mine, Marge, but of course I understand – and I have far worse things to tell you. I met a girl called Mildred at a party in Narvik some months ago. We had a pleasant enough evening but it was nothing special as far as I was concerned. However, she had other ideas and was determined to achieve her goal. To cut a long story short, she is pregnant and there is enormous pressure from her and her entire family for me to marry her. You can probably imagine the situation, it's a small community. I feel trapped totally. I am so deeply sorry to have to tell you this."

My heart sank lower and lower as I heard the story. "I don't know how all this is going to end, Marge, but I want you to know that it is *you* I love."

I managed a smile and said, "I guess we'll just have to wait and see but I'll always be here for you, Odd, always. This 'connection' we have, I have every faith in *us*."

The next letter from Oslo, dated July 1953 sums up the intensity of the situation.

Dear, dear Marge

It is not so far between us. As long as I can imagine the distance and the landscape I feel as if we are close together.

I don't need to recall our meeting to my mind. Every second of it is here. From the first moment in Oxford Street to the incredibly sad and depressing departure when a taxi carried you away from me. Oh, Marge, if it is going to continue like this, it will be Hell. Hell on earth.

I really don't dare to think of the future. The way seems too dark and cruel. And I am frightened, yes, I am frightened. But I am not going to give in. I am not bitter. I only feel sore. My heart is a sore and aching spot – and my eyes are empty. I feel like seeing beyond and through people.

Tomorrow I fly northward – to Bodø – where I probably will meet Mildred. And here it starts again. The pain – and the longing, I can't face it, Marge. And I am so sorry to think of the awful time you must have. In a way I brought you into it. I just wonder how you are getting on with your Mother. If she can't understand this, Marge, you had better not tell her anything about us.

Also, I sincerely hope you have forgotten the 'awkward' situation on leaving Rose Court. What do they know of the *beauty* that we felt together – even if we had to steal it all? And what is more important than beauty and happiness?

I am sitting right now in a restaurant in the centre of Oslo alone – almost. I couldn't stay at home; the walls call out and reflect my fantastic longing and loneliness.

There is music around me – soft. But where are your eyes, Marge? Those I loved to look at. Where are your hands – your smile? And the childlike playing atmosphere that made every moment worthwhile.

I can't understand that I am of the same race as these human beings around me here. They are foreign to me – like distant planets. There are only two human beings in our world – you and me.

It hurts me terribly to think that I can't get any letters from you for a while – but do write what you feel and send it to me later when there is an opportunity.

You must not expect to hear too often from me either. Later from the end of August, we can correspond again. Everything is indeed relative. Now even a letter seems a precious link between us – it is like a prison where you look forward to an escape. It is terrible Marge – and I long for you so much. Whenever I feel blue, I'll think of our beautiful meetings – and I am sure it will help. It was like champagne.

Take care of yourself darling and have courage. What matters is that we love each other – beyond prison and time and distance.

I'll tell you later when you can write.

With my heart blood

Yours, Odd

I had to wait nearly eight weeks for the next letter.

Oslo, September 14th 1953

Dearest Marge

I am really sorry that I have not been able to write before. It has worried me a lot. But it has been so difficult and I have not been mentally and emotionally mature and prepared to establish the contact with you again – however much I have wanted to.

Yes, it is over now. I have changed my status. I am a married man. Please excuse me if I do not go into details.

You will understand I know.

But something must be told. When I met Mildred in Bodø in July (it was an appointment to meet before I went home) we had a rather delicate problem to handle. I was determined not to tell her about you. Not yet. But she was intelligent enough to sort of feel how things stood. Eventually I told her how we met again in London – and that I loved you and not her – but would still marry her because of the child.

It was terrible, Marge, I had a terrible time. We both had (and what about you, darling?).

It appeared in the discussion that there was another argument in favour of marriage, according to Mildred. She said no teacher with a child *outside* of marriage is allowed to teach in Norway (a divorced one can of course).

The marriage took place at her place – and very many guests were invited. I can't tell about it.

Then, before I left Narvik, I became ill – so my departure was delayed but since September 1st, I have been here where the course I am attending is in full progress. It is good to be active, to study. It helps matters.

But nothing can help my state of mind – and my troubled heart. The situation seems to me fantastic. Mildred in Narvik, you darling in London and I am in Oslo. I do not know what you feel – but if you *are* the same as before – it must be a pretty hard time for you.

Mildred is awaiting a baby in November and she is very nervous, perhaps understanding with her heart what she has to face in the immediate future. And I, lonely and depressed here in Oslo – having nothing else to do but to *wait*. There is nothing we can do but wait right now. It is cruel, and my impatience is like disease in my blood.

I think and think – and sometimes I am afraid I am doing the wrong thing by keeping you like this. Please darling write soon and tell me everything. Where you are, what you do, how you feel, if you have changed – and what your plans are.

I sort of dislike writing more until I hear from you. I am so eager to hear from you. So please let me know immediately.

You remember we talked about you coming to Oslo. What about it? Or what is the situation with your Mother? Of course you have to pay all attention to her. But the mere thought of you here makes me crazy.

I am staying with relations here in Oslo – so please address your letter to Post Restante, Oslo, and I will collect the letter there. You understand.

It is autumn in Oslo. With a high sky and bleeding trees. It is all a feast of Nature. At the weekends I stroll around in the woods north of Oslo – and guess what I feel and think?

I miss you Marge, and every minute we had together in London I bring with me. They were all so vital. I am turning crazy at the thought of how things could have been – and if only I had gone to Australia earlier.

Dear Marge, all my love to you and I am counting the hours till I hear from you.

Yours, Odd

"Incidentally that story of Mildred's that if you had a child outside marriage, you were not allowed to teach in Norway, turned out to be a load of nonsense. I don't think I can cope with anymore letters today, Marge. Let's take the car and go out for a while."

"Great idea," I said.

Chapter 4

We needed some provisions so we decided to go to the supermarket. Odd's first purchase was a big bunch of beautiful red roses.

"These are for you, Mrs Irtun."

"Wow!" I exclaimed. "I've made it at last, have I?" We both laughed.

"Perhaps I should have said Mrs Irfield."

"Or," I suggested, "Mrs Bloomtun?"

"No," Odd said. "My preference is Mrs Irtunfield." We wandered around the supermarket, hand in hand, like a pair of lovesick teenagers on their first date. Shopping completed, we returned to the car to discover that Odd had a heavy fine to pay. Unbelievably we had parked the car right under the sign that said "No Parking". Our craziness didn't stop there either. Odd decided the car needed a good clean so off we went to the carwash. I commented that I had never been in a car in a carwash before. So Odd said, "Then I think we should make it memorable…" and we did!

Back at the flat, he needed his afternoon nap, something which he had found necessary since his illness. I have never been able to sleep during the day but, at his request, I cuddled him to sleep, his head on my chest. Now I had to do my best to lie quietly, lost in my thoughts. I looked long and hard at this dear man lying beside me, this man who so completely broke my heart all those years ago. After 20 minutes or so, the heat from his enveloping body was becoming too much for me. Mustering all the stealth I could manage, I slipped out of bed and went to the kitchen to busy myself with preparations for dinner.

Half an hour later Odd emerged. "I woke up to discover you had left me, Marge" he said in an accusing voice. "Makes a change" I retorted acidly – and then gave him a warm smile.

Secretly, I had to admit to myself that I was still rather wary – and no wonder!

It was time for our evening aperitif – and some music. Odd had a wonderful collection of classical CDs including some opera. We had such similar tastes in music – as in so many other areas of our lives. Each hour it seemed we uncovered something remembered or something new and interesting about each other – and so much in common. It was just the way I remembered our relationship – and here we were again after all these years rediscovering the past and wholeheartedly enjoying the present but with an enhanced awareness. Looked at from the outside, I guess we were just a pair of 'old timers' BUT capable of making each other feel all the same explosive sensations that we felt in our twenties. "You make me shiver, Marge, you always did." My way of expressing our affinity was that his nearness, his touch gave me 'electric shocks'. Shivers or shocks, it was all so – beautiful. The word is insufficient, I fear, a bit like saying fire is hot or water is wet.

"How about reading some more letters?" I asked.

"Why not!"

September 30th 1953

Dearest Marge

I have just collected your very dear letters and the photos that bring back clearer than anything the sad and happy London stay.

And I am sending this in all haste to break the interlude – the real letter comes soon. I didn't expect your letters to arrive so quickly, imagine my surprise when I collected three letters all at once. It was wonderful. I read them in the middle of the street with cars and trams almost running me down! It was like the wanderer in the desert who finally found water.

What a peculiar life – and yet it is what you make it. In spite of all we have been through, I try to be happy – I try to smile because after all you exist in the same world as I do – and our experience together nobody can take from us. It will always live – those memories of living intensely. Only the future can tell us what we shall share of happiness but we will fight for it – and not give in.

I miss you terribly darling. It is always there. I am split in two. Half of my attention is always in London.

I am so glad to hear that you get along well with your Mother, and that you are taking up a course at the university.

Dear Marge, I am always yours, Odd

The longer letter followed on the:

Oslo, October 1ˢᵗ 1953

Dear Marge

With your precious letters and a bundle of photos in front of me, I am myself a picture – of what? Of loneliness and despair, of uncertainty and longing. Yes the two last factors are predominant. It is raining heavily outside – autumn weather – and it is autumn here too.

And in these photos you smile and we smile. It seems so long ago. It was our summer – a short and hectic one. I must believe it happened for they are here, all the memories – even nicer on the paper, a materialised dream.

My thoughts stop here – I cannot face reality. The hopeless reality that you are there – and I am here – with a high wall between – and the only thing we can do is wait. I have not got the patience! I cannot stand the thought of playing this part to its ultimate end – this depressing part for an ignorant audience. And yet there is nothing else to do! What a wonderful creation man is. What an ability to adapt. But my word it costs!

It is as if there is nothing left inside me – as if I were hollow, deaf and dumb. Partly of frustration and partly of self-reproach. It is drawing on the mental sources. Whatever I do, I feel the pressure of this terrific dilemma on me. I know there are many unhappy people in the world at this moment. Maybe my problems are scarcely vital compared with those. Still, each individual is a world of its own – and my little world is in a dangerous state.

You see, Marge, I thought I was sufficiently tough to not give a damn about others – but I can't. That is why I have acted as I did. That is why I can't be with you right now. In spite of your protests, Marge, I admire you intensely for your attitude. For your faith in love and us. It is so positive and hopeful that it is bound to bear fruits.

I have read with great interest your account of the dramatic settlement with your Mother. I am not quite sure whether you were right to tell her *everything* ... although in the long run, it might be useful for her to face all this. I am also glad to hear that her opinion about me is positive. I wouldn't hesitate for a moment telling her that my connection with you has been sincere and not meant to involve you in any troubles or difficulties – you know that. In fact I will always suffer from the fact that I am sort of 'holding you' in this period. But you have of course your obvious right to do what you want and make your exit when it suits you (which I hope I will never hear!).

I guess you will be back in London now after your trip and I do hope you had a good time with your Mother before she leaves for Australia. I can hardly believe that you are staying on – and with the positive 'consent' of the family.

Your plans to take up studies appeals to me also. Instead of philosophy I would suggest psychology (or perhaps both) – and French – along with European literature (modern) –

French and English. But there will hardly be time for it all.

I can see you in your room in Phillimore Gardens with that view over the park – and my heart aches. Why? Wouldn't it be wonderful to live there together – with you and music and studies? (The gin one has to abandon when studying and the consumption of tobacco must be greatly reduced).

I feel I am getting encouraged when I next approach this delicate question: you and Oslo – when your Mother has left. But there are so many 'buts' which you know as well as I. The studies of yours, the unpleasant season here in November and, of course, the financial position. Personally, I am in such a bad state economically that I am unable to help you in case you come to Oslo. But what a wonderful thing to think of! So many things we have to talk about and experience together! However I can't suggest anything – it only remains for me to hope.

My course at the university will last until the middle of December. It comprises practical teaching at high schools, pedagogic theory, psychology and methods of teaching. It is pretty hard work with teaching in the morning and lectures in the afternoon. As I am living about half an hour by train outside of Oslo (a township called Lillestrøm), I am quite exhausted by the time I come home at night.

It is hard to look into the future – but as I have got to face it, I can as well tell you. About Christmastime, I shall have to go north to Narvik. By that time, Mildred will have had the baby (sometime around the middle of November).

Afterwards, I am taking a job somewhere near or in Oslo

with the intention to study as well at the university. I think of taking up English literature again. It is very hard to get a flat here – so the chances of bringing Mildred and the baby down here will be minimal. Maybe when the baby is a few months older it can stay with her parents and Mildred can take some kind of a job down here. The only thing to do I feel is to live with Mildred for some time to find out what it is like. Then I will have the chance to say "No, this does not work. I want a divorce". It sounds very brutal but I can't, without trying it, claim a divorce. I must think of her parents – and mine too! If by living together for a few months we find it is impossible, it would be easier to break off. I believe Mildred is prepared for the worst. In one of her letters, she alluded to you but she did not want to ask any questions she said. I am not telling her about our correspondence. Not yet. She has a bad enough time.

And next summer maybe I'll take a trip to London again – but that is very far off. What will have happened by July 1954 when perhaps you return home? A world of wonders! By the way, what chances are there in Australia to get a job do you think? (A question I should have put at least one year ago). It is especially in the field of teaching I am interested.

I am yours, I miss you, I want you – and I wonder so much what you are doing right now? I hope you are writing and thinking of always yours, Odd

"Playing the waiting game in London was hell for me too you know."

"Yes, Marge, I know it was. I was well aware of it."

"Thinking back to April 5th 1953, it felt as if my life was 'on hold', it was almost as if I was permanently holding my breath. I recall, Odd, that we discussed endlessly how best to deal with our situation. Finally we agreed that we would try and carry on with our lives as normally as possible. Remember those discussions? We both had our studies, which gave a measure of stability, and we would go out with friends of course – date even, if either of us wanted to, because it wouldn't mean anything. We had our big secret, our love for each other, which we knew would allow us to be together one day, no matter how long we had to wait." (Little did I think it would take this long!) Odd looked thoughtful – but said nothing.

I decided not to pursue this topic, but I remembered so vividly – in spite of all the obstacles – how positive I felt about the future – well, most of the time anyway. On my occasional bad days, doubts would creep in as I pondered the whole absurd situation. What was I doing? How did I get myself into this no man's land of uncertainty? The constant longing, of which we both wrote, was at times unbearable. How much of this craziness could I tolerate? Then I would close my eyes and hear Odd's voice repeating over and over again: "What matters is that we love each other."

At last Odd broke the silence. "You know I wish – especially now – that I had not got rid of your letters. They were pearls of beauty. You always sounded so strong in them, so full of faith in us. Your letters kept me going, particularly when I sank into one of my bouts of depression. As you know, I have tended towards melancholy all my life."

"Yes, I know you have. My Robert was the same. I think highly sensitive people often struggle with depression. However, the other side of the coin, Odd, is that your extreme sensitivity has helped to make you a wonderful poet – and a highly acclaimed one too."

"Perhaps" he shrugged.

"How about another letter – but just read me the interesting bits."

November 2nd 1953

Dearest Marge

I think of you every day and I know it must be lonely now as your Mother has left. I have tried to imagine what that departure looked like. What a moment full of wonder and unasked questions for both of you.

If only I were there to take care of you – to go out, discuss and live with you. To love you. If ... if ... and what are you doing with yourself now darling?

It is another eternity since I saw your blue envelope – I know that letter by heart – and I am longing for new nourishment for a hungry soul.

Personally I should have written before now – but you know that depression ... it is better now. But one day I was quite sick and couldn't teach.

Did I tell you that I intend to apply for a position in the Foreign Service – Mildred does not like the idea as she knows there are minimal chances to get a flat in Oslo. Besides she is rather ill at the moment. The types of blood we have, have caused a sort of poison in her blood. Consequently there is quite a danger for the child. So these days she is going to the hospital and in a few days I expect we shall know the result. It is not at all pleasant.

There is so much I want to say, but it is so difficult in my present position. So I'll mainly tell you about the exterior things – and leave it to you to read between the lines.

It is quite a strain at the moment, teaching in the morning, taking a train to Oslo, then read and attend lectures in the evenings plus adult lessons in English which I give twice a week. Still there are many spare moments for *dreaming*. I am always in your room in London. I liked that. That atmosphere with you and the lights from the top floor of London inspired me. It melted together to an essence of red life – red as the heart blood itself.

And those pub moments we had! The walks – and the intense moments in my room – I would give much to have you here and now.

What about it?

You know how I long for you, how intensely I desire you. And what a heaven it might have been … But I also know the practical difficulties – the finance, the rain and darkness here – all is so difficult. But still how beautiful it might have been. If I get a job in Oslo after Christmas we might have a chance then to meet here.

Darling why is it so? But we must not give up for a moment. We must continue to believe. Think of all the activities we shall share – all the beauty we shall experience – all the love we shall meet. Think of all the days and nights that are still ahead. They are still unwritten and we'll fill them with a poem, a love song – because the days and nights ought to be a play, light and gay.

Tell me *all* about yourself darling – what you do and think, with whom you go out, what you read. Tell me about your longing, it is still there?

Dearest Marge, I am waiting for your letter. Maybe it contains the unbelievable thing – the fantastic dream that after all you can find your way here!

In any case I am waiting for your next letter – and my life is full of you.

With all my love

Yours, Odd

Oslo, November 10th 1953

Dear Marge

I do understand you so well – and I have been through the same process of doubt and longing, practical objections and that intense feeling of the necessity of seeing you.

I have been through it for weeks and it is a waste of time going into details as I know darling you have been through the same.

The only and very sad difference is that I have come to a conclusion. *I do not think you should come here right now Marge!*

It is terrible to say it, to think of it, not seeing you for another long time perhaps.

Personally I am not able to come to you before Xmas.

The exams take place from December 14th-17th and that leaves no interval for a London trip.

But what is going to happen after the Holy Christmas? Only the gods know. My intention is to get a job in Oslo so I can study as well. Most probably I'll live *alone*. Maybe then … we will have the chance.

I am not going to see you soon, that marvellous thought I have played with day and night. All we were going to say and do – all the love that finally would find expression, near and warm!

It is not necessary to give the reasons – you indicated most of them in your letter. Besides I am so afraid that the *beauty* between us would be destroyed due to all these … practical things, trivial banalities. We must *not* destroy the beauty, Marge, that binds us together.

When the conditions are better, we will experience it again – see it thrive and grow like a flower – and we'll forget all the rest.

In the meantime we have to develop ourselves. You with your studies, which I hope you enjoy and derive benefit. And I continue with mine – and my daydream, my constant longing for you. There is so much to learn and to take an interest in. We can *share* all that once we get together. It will make life rich and colourful. Life is more than domestic affairs and bread and butter. And we'll prove it! These are big words perhaps but I take them damn seriously! Meantime I continue with my dreams about you and me (and gin and music and your soft skin against mine!).

I'll write again soon darling. Promise to be a good girl – even if etc.

Jeg elsker deg! Remember?

I see you in that costume – the black beret, the blouse and skirt – and my heart is tender with longing.

Yours, Odd

"Enough letters for tonight, let's have some dinner," Odd suggested, "and put on some music – opera perhaps. I would like to hear you sing, Marge."

When I was nursing Robert he liked me to sing to him which I did gladly. When he died I lost my singing voice completely. I had told Odd this some weeks back in one of our long telephone conversations and he was determined to get me singing again. Whilst preparing dinner we sang a duet – my voice was indeed coming back, I could hardly believe it! Of course it helped to sing with someone – and Odd had a lovely singing voice – and a wonderful speaking voice too. It was probably one of the first things that attracted me to him all those years ago. It was rich and deep with just that touch of accent that made it very sexy. "Marge, did you notice a change in your speaking voice as well? I seem to remember it used to be a bit stronger and deeper."

"Yes you are right. I must try to remember to lower it."

Chapter 5

"You, Marge, are the world's best kisser! Everything you do, you do so well."

"I'm glad you think so," I replied.

"I had rather given up on kissing, I thought it became inappropriate ... as one grew older."

"What rubbish" I retorted. "If one is young at heart – and we are – then nothing is inappropriate."

"You are right – *again*," he grinned. "The sun is shining, let's go out for the day. There is a wonderful museum of music, set in delightful parkland on the outskirts of Trondheim. We'll go by car."

Driving with Odd was a rather special experience. I thought he'd put kangaroo juice in the car, the way it leapt along but he loved to be behind the wheel and seemed to enjoy speed. In no time at all(!) we arrived at our destination. It was indeed a beautiful park and, with sunshine in abundance, we decided to skip the museum and spend the day out-of-doors. We lunched on the terrace of the museum's restaurant and spent the afternoon strolling around the park talking – not only to each other but to everyone we came across. He was interested in everything and everyone and wherever we went he would talk to people, engage with them, draw them out, make them feel important. He had an astonishing alchemy for making those he met feel truly valued.

As the sun was setting, we made our way home in time for the evening's aperitif and some music. There was a particular CD Odd had in his collection called "Secret Garden" which became 'our special music' just as, all those years ago, there was a piece called "Ebbtide" which we had called 'ours'. "Secret Garden" can express the inexpressible, it is very moving and romantic, mystical even, especially the third piece. We played it often.

Out of the blue, Odd suddenly said, "You are perfick Mrs Larkin." Obviously he had been a fan of "The Darling Buds of May" which had been shown on Norwegian television. It was a phrase he repeated frequently and I loved it – especially the look on his face that went with it. But now it was time for another letter.

Oslo, November 20ᵗʰ 1953
Dearest Marge

What an avalanche of feelings! Right through me – and it was just an ordinary letter with blue envelope – but the blueness was like the August sky. How often did I ask for that sky? Every day I stood in front of the Post Restante Department with the same question. The lady behind the counter at last took a personal interest in me – probably she was as glad as I was yesterday when my expectations were not frustrated.

I am so in love with your letters, Marge – and it strikes me that I didn't think of that before. You should have attended that journalistic course! Your style is so essential and living that it should be enjoyed by a greater audience than only little me. (Of course I know that you have some other selected few!) I hope you will be able to get into one of the classes in journalism later on.

But this was all a digression. I am as thirsty as you are for news but from now on please write to my address below. It is such a nuisance to apply to the Post Office every day but I can't help it! I go there every day! My relatives may think what they like. I have not told them anything about you and me. One day they will know anyhow!

How I love your honesty – and how I appreciate that you tell me all your thoughts and fears. You can imagine that I also have my ups and downs. How vital it is to have your love and your faith to drink from. They are sources of *beauty* that my soul craves.

Marge, as you know, your letter contained a note from your Mother. I can't begin to express my feelings when I read it. It was a very vital message to me and very inspiring – even more so because I realise the depression she must have been through to be able to adopt this *tolerant* attitude towards me. Her letter meant a great deal to me and I want you to explain that to her. It gave me in a way force and strength. You must bring her my most sincere regards and I hope she left Europe without bitterness – and with the confidence that I personally will do whatever I can to make you happy. You Marge. I'll write to her later on – and explain my position.

Dearest Marge I have to finish off now – but the link is there always irrespective of the North Sea – and everything else.

Yours always, Odd

November 27ᵗʰ 1953
Dearest Marge

Why didn't I write to you before? I am sorry I have kept you waiting but there has been nothing to say – and still nothing to tell. The baby seems to be late – it should have been born 12 days ago as far as I have been told – but I have not heard a word from Narvik for quite a long time. As far as I know Mildred is alright – and it quite often happens that the birth takes place a fortnight later than it ought to.

Still it has been a hell of a time as you can imagine and the thoughts and the worries do not give me a moment's rest. Marge, it is no use describing and painting in rich colours all the things one feels and everything that enters one's mind so that one often feels quite ashamed of oneself. I suppose it is all human – I suppose I am not worse than anybody else. It is just that I want you so much – want to be with you day and night. I want your friendship, your company, your love.

Sometimes in the street among all the unknown white faces, I see *you*. And I long so intensely to walk alongside you, looking at shop windows together, smiling at the same things and I want to stretch out my hand, knowing that you are there. Or, to be in your room with all its atmosphere – just lying on the sofa and looking at you reading "with a song in my heart".

What is happening in a few days I have to accept – though you must understand I do not like it.

In two days I will have finished my teaching at the high school then follows, the exams. Probably I will be leaving Oslo on Dec 18th. Still I do not know the result of my application to the Foreign Service.

It will be a short letter this time, I will write again as soon as it has happened. It can't take more than 2-3 days now.

Dearest Marge, I can't express my longing and my warmth in a letter. But you are with me all the time. Please write as often as you can.

Always yours, Odd

When the next letter arrived, it was in a pink envelope. I recall vividly that I could not bring myself to open it for some 10 minutes or so. I remember asking myself – So what do you think about your man now? Not only does he have a wife, but now he has a baby daughter as well. The answer came loud and clear, however long it takes, I'll wait for him. I guess that's what's called unconditional love. Of course knowing how much he loved me made the waiting game tolerable.

Oslo, December 5th 1953
Darling

Yes Marge – it has happened now. On December 2nd (17 days late). It's a girl according to the telegram – and everything was alright. I have not heard anything since so I suppose everything continues to be alright.

What did I feel in the moment I received the news? I think I have not yet realised what has happened. I cannot grasp it – and at the same time I feel I am making it more difficult than necessary.

After all it is better to have a definite result instead of the dreadful period of constant waiting. You have felt how it was I am sure – just as you seem to feel in harmony with everything else.

It is a definite result – I have only got to act accordingly in the immediate future. It is going to be hard – for all of us – and my heart aches for you, so far away.

I am not happy. I feel I am choking with difficulties – but life has to go on. One has to cling to hope – and be patient. After all it cannot take too long a time before a decision has to be taken.

Regarding the future plans here in Norway, I am going to return to Oslo immediately after Xmas –and it is very likely that I am going to be alone.

I hate to think that you are celebrating your Christmas 'alone' in London. My thoughts will be there all the time. I am afraid I will not be able to write to you during that period either.

Darling, you don't say anything, but I feel your presence. Do you remember that night in Chelsea? Happy like a dream. Crazy like love itself. "There is a song in my heart" – the orchestra plays it right now.

Your letters are getting deeper and deeper and I love them dearly because they are the best substitute for you (if you have any?). Oh my 'childish' desire for happiness that I am so sure of experiencing with you. I am so in the mood for you right now – more than ever (I am almost breaking the fountain pen!).

And what am I facing? Studies, and there is a hell of a lot to plough through.

It is good to hear that you are able to concentrate on your studies – and I like your absolute claims to happiness by shooing away the queue of admiring men!

I am glad you are willing to help me with my playwright, James Bridie. I long for the day we can cooperate in things like that – just imagine Marge – oh my blood gets hot!

My dearest Marge, I am sick of being lonely.

Yours, Odd

"That seems like a good point to stop our letter-reading for tonight. However, as I don't have any of your letters, Marge, tell me instead about what was going on in your life at that time."

"Heavens, where do I start?"

"How about at the beginning?"

"Right, let me gather my thoughts. When I first met you, Odd, in 1951, I was on that world trip with my Mother. As she was accustomed to comfort, we did everything in style. However, when I returned to Europe in 1953, I was determined to do things differently. By then I was financially independent as some years before, my Father had given me and my sister a large number of shares in his business. In the fullness of time, the shares did very well and, as a result, I had rather a lot of money at my disposal. I was not interested in investing it. I just wanted to blow the lot on travelling. I reasoned that if I travelled 'cattle class' and stayed in modest accommodation then my funds could last rather a long time.

When I ran out of cash, I told myself that would be time enough to settle down and find myself some meaningful occupation. I had such a hunger for everything life had to offer that it seemed the best way to spend my money was on living abroad – wherever my travels might take me. I was also keen to study and, in general, find out what the big wide world was all about.

In addition you, Odd, were hovering in the background – whatever that might – or might not – mean. You will recall that we wrote to each other very regularly when I was back in Australia. Of course when we said goodbye in 1951, we didn't know if we would ever meet again but, deep down, we both dreamt that it would happen – and happen it did.

Just after I had booked my passage back to the UK, my Mother decided that she too would like to come, provided she could be in London in time for the Coronation of Queen Elizabeth II AND be able to see something of the pageantry. I was working at the time as P.A. to the Merchandise Manager of a high-fashion store in Melbourne. Because the store had agents in London, my boss was able to organise some splendid tickets for us to view the Coronation procession from the windows of Peter Robinson, a store that was then right on the corner of Oxford Circus. In addition, there was a champagne buffet and, more importantly, television which allowed us to see as well the action that wasn't passing before us.

A few weeks later, Mother's deep affection for all things Royal was further enriched by our invitation to attend a Royal Garden Party. It was a fascinating day seeing inside Buckingham Palace and its beautiful gardens, not to mention being in close proximity to the Royal Family. I was particularly pleased to bump into (quite literally) the actor, John Mills, with whom I had a very jolly conversation. Of course famous faces were in abundance that day."

"I am going to make us a coffee, but don't stop. I love your reminiscences. How about some memories from the other side of the Channel, Marge."

"As you wish, let's see, I'll start with Paris. On a visit to that beautiful city with Mother, we went one evening to a quaint little restaurant called "Grenouille" on the Left Bank. It was tucked away up a lane – and full of surprises. It was long and narrow with a central aisle and tables for four either side. There were no menus, instead the choice of dishes was written on a blackboard at the end of the restaurant and each table was provided with binoculars in order to see what was on offer. It was all noisy, friendly and informal. All the diners talked to each other and even swapped forkfuls of food. We got chatting to the three men at the table opposite ours; they all spoke fluent English. One was a Belgian airline pilot, another an Italian count and the third a French theatrical agent.

At the end of a highly amusing and rather boozy meal, the trio invited us to join them at a nearby existentialist cellar club where the jazz, they said, was sensational. We were outside in the lane talking when one of them burst into song – and we all joined in. I guess we were making rather a lot of noise and, in retaliation, a window above us opened and someone emptied a chamber pot full of pee which landed in full force on my Mother. She was not amused, poor darling, but we could not stop laughing. We mopped her up as best we could with handkerchiefs and assured her she would soon dry out. Of course Mother would have preferred to go straight back to our hotel and have a bath but she was not going to leave me with three men we had only just met.

Once inside the cellar club, the considerable heat did indeed begin to dry her out – but the smell was awful so we had to seat poor Mummie on the far side of the table, as far away as possible from the rest of us. As the evening progressed her clothes were smelling to high heaven so, with reluctance, we left. One way and another it was a memorable evening.

I have just remembered some Italian episodes. These actually happened in 1951, only a few weeks after I met you, Odd, but I don't think I told you about them. We were travelling by train to Venice. An hour or so into the journey, the train stopped at a large station. Mother said she was rather hungry. I looked out our carriage window and could see, much further along the platform, a man with a food trolley doing a brisk trade with the passengers. We dashed through the train to where the action was and I bought a couple of sandwiches. Just as I was paying, there was a loud noise and the train lurched. I quickly realised that the train had come apart and the half we were on was going slowly in one direction whilst the other half – *with all our luggage* – was going in the opposite direction! We jumped off the train and I waved frantically to the Guard. After much Italian histrionics, the train stopped and we were allowed to get back on the right part and rejoin our luggage. Unfortunately Mother had to remain hungry as I had dropped the sandwiches on the platform in all the excitement.

During our three-day visit to Venice, I met a handsome Italian guy."

"Why does that not surprise me, Marge. Remembering what that young blonde Australian with the hour glass figure did to this polar bear, I can well imagine how an ardent Italian would react."

"Be that as it may. He was very kind. Showed us the sights, took us out to dinner and so on but communication was very difficult. His English was as poor as my Italian. Of course one can always manage somehow with a dictionary and sign language.

As we were leaving he asked for my address. Then, rather to my surprise, Mother said 'We'll let you know when we are coming back. Venice is so captivating, we must come here again.' Over the next few weeks I received several letters from him but they were difficult to understand. I remember on one occasion lunching at an Italian restaurant in London and asking the waiter if he could just give me the gist of what was expressed. A big grin crept over his face as he read – 'I think this man, Virgilio, is in love with you' he said.

In September we did indeed make another trip to Italy, arriving in Venice, as it happened, right on my birthday. Virgilio met us at the station and almost immediately he gave me a present. It was a ring which he slipped on to the third finger of my right hand. I assumed it was a birthday gift and thanked him warmly.

The following day Mother wanted to go shopping so Virgilio took me to the Lido for the day. Armed with dictionaries once again, I was astonished to discover that he considered we were engaged to be married! I had no idea that Italians wore engagement rings on the *right* hand. I returned the ring immediately and apologised for the confusion. He looked very sad but insisted that I must keep the ring as a souvenir of Venice. I still have it.

One last story for tonight. This one is a little Spanish cameo. At the hotel I was staying at in Granada, there was a group of gypsy flamenco dancers providing some entertainment in the bar. After the performance, I met a couple of them, a brother and sister. She had just appeared in a film as a Spanish dancer. He was quite a charmer and sheer magic on the guitar.

My bedroom on the first floor had a little balcony overlooking the courtyard. Imagine my surprise when I went upstairs to bed and found Miguel under my balcony playing the guitar to me and singing a haunting love song. In my opinion Spanish experiences don't get much better than that! They invited me for a drink the next day in their cave. As I had never sipped sherry with a gypsy before in a cave, I felt this was not to be missed . The word cave is misleading – yes, the dwellings are built into the rock-face but they are very well equipped caves. Whitewashed walls, electric light, and charmingly furnished. No windows of course but apart from that, a des. res., I would say!"

"Well I think that's enough memories for tonight, Marge. Besides, I now want to seduce you."

"Really, that's if I don't seduce you first."

Chapter 6

"It's another beautiful day, Marge – perfect for a stroll by the river, with perhaps a stop for refreshment at one of the harbour cafés?"

"Sounds great." Of course I would have been happy doing anything – or nothing – as long as we were together. Life felt as if we had been dipped in serotonin, the happiness substance. I suppose there was an element of living each day as if it was the last. Odd's serious illness undoubtedly added a certain poignancy, another dimension I guess, to the relationship we were now enjoying.

In the midst of making breakfast, Odd turned to me and said, "You would have made a wonderful wife, Marge." Now you tell me, I thought to myself but said out loud, "Oh I did, as a matter of fact – twice – or so I was told," then added with a grin, "but you'll just have to take my word for it." I guess we were two people with a lot of love to give and, although we had given so much over the years to our respective partners, we still had one hell of a lot left for each other – here and now.

On our way to the harbour we called into a couple of galleries. It never ceased to amaze how similar our tastes were, not only in the arts, but virtually in every aspect of life, we seemed to be in harmony. It was such an extraordinary sense of belonging – even after all those silent years, and not forgetting for a moment that we both had very happy marriages. Of course, we were able to talk freely and openly about our spouses, indeed there wasn't a subject we couldn't discuss. He asked me who was the love of my life – Tom or Robert? Without hesitation, I replied, "Robert" – then silently I asked myself – so where does Odd fit in? Where indeed! Perhaps the answer is "in a unique category all his own". Whatever it was that we had found in each other in our twenties, it had survived over time, distance and every other component of life's colourful tapestry. Not only had it survived, it was intact and as strong as ever.

The day passed happily and soon we made our way home for some supper, not that Odd was interested in food. But that to one side, he was not in any pain and he was in great spirits. His wretched disease was behaving quite well at the moment, although for how long, nobody knew.

"So what news did my next letter bring?" he asked.

"In spite of your warning that you would not be able to write to me over the so-called Festive Season, you did in fact manage it."

The first day of the New Year
Darling
    Finally – I know how you must feel, and I feel for you so much. I must try to be practical and record what

has happened…

I left Oslo on Dec 19th. Oh what thoughts! Can you imagine? I saw *you* all the time. I 'celebrated' Xmas with Mildred outside Narvik – and now I am visiting my parents. It is all too fantastic – a play. "Life is a tragedy to the man who feels and a comedy to the man who thinks" – it often enters my mind.

It was not a happy reunion. I suppose I couldn't conceal the truth well enough. But the strain to keep up an official façade!

The baby girl is very nice – which even I could recognise – and it means a lot to Mildred. But I am afraid I have disappointed her dreadfully by controlling my enthusiasm to the degree I have.

It is all beyond words – a constant suffering – and I think Mildred is well aware of the coming tragedy. I can't continue with this.

It is four o'clock in the morning after a little party at home with old school friends – six of whom are now doctors. We have had too much to drink. But all the time I am wondering about you darling, what you are doing and what the New Year has in its lap – for *us*.

My plans are to return to Oslo about the middle of January and I hope that will bring me closer to a meeting with you. I hope that can be realised. It must be darling. How I wonder what you have been doing this Xmas and NY Eve. I look to the future as the living hope.

Darling, dearest. You know how I miss you and long for

you. I'll write again as soon as I can.

The books on Bridie are very valuable and I am grateful indeed for your assistance.

Don't you feel how I think of you?

Yours, Odd

P.S. New Year's Eve – endless streams of thoughts were sent off to you – with tender feelings.

Oslo, January 27th 1954

Marge darling

What must you be feeling, darling! I have tried to figure that out from the depth of my own depressed feelings. But I could not possibly write before. I arrived in Oslo last night. I was delayed up there. Mildred took ill, rather seriously, and I had to stay on.

And what has happened, darling? I am here alone. The idea is that I am going to write a thesis – and back home, Mildred is staying with the baby as I cannot afford to have her here, nor provide the young family with a flat. That is the exterior situation. The inner self is a bloody mess. A constant battle between all sorts of forces. I know you understand me, darling. That is the great thing. There are all sorts of feelings: the drive to follow the social sense of duty – and the much stronger one to fight for a lifelong striving for happiness. It would be simple if things were ordinary but, you see, Mildred is mad. Or rather, she will be if anything happens. I am afraid so. She has got a terrific temperament, shaped for a sort of life-denying line, if anything important to her fails – I have seen it.

But still – how long is one going to bring sacrifices to the altar of Convention and Duty and Society?

That is why I can't use the big knife at once and just cut.

We talked about divorce. We did not talk about *you*. But she must know. She has a penetrating intuition – and she has not much faith. That is how it is.

But how long is it going to take? Darling, I cannot answer now. Possibly she is coming down here in April/May.

Has the baby changed anything? It is difficult to answer. It is certain that my very reserved attitude towards it was an extremely big disappointment to Mildred – and my feelings towards the baby are not very warm either, even if I could see that the baby is very nice and well-shaped. But you must guess my thoughts, Marge – and besides, this must be torture for you to read, so I will stop here.

(There are then a couple of paragraphs about James Bridie, which I shall skip.)

This brings my mind to the burning question that I cannot push back any longer – it has been in the pen all the time!

What about it? Can you possibly do Norway the honour? It is now only a practical problem. Darling, these feelings are so difficult to control – and the longing is so red and warm. I dare not imagine how it would be.

You are always with me.

Yours, Odd

"Odd, I don't think I am going to read every single word of your letters, nor for that matter every letter. There are so many of them."

"I agree, Marge. They get a bit samey don't they?"

"Well, I guess there is a finite number of ways a guy can tell a gal how much he loves her."

"And I seem to have covered that subject rather well. Nevertheless I would like to have photocopies of all the letters so that I can read and digest them at leisure."

"Sure, no problem. I'll get them photocopied as soon as I return home – and post them to you."

"Oh, no, I want personal delivery please. Either you come back here, or I'll come to you."

"So you view our relationship rediscovery programme as ongoing do you?"

"Indeed I do, Marge – and I am not going to let you go this time."

At this point I was tempted to fix him with an icy stare and insist on hearing exactly *why* he left me before. In spite of all our difficulties there was always the certainty that we belonged to each other and would be together one day. On reflection, I decided that such confrontations rarely yield a meaningful result. If he wanted to tell me, eventually he would. And if he didn't want to, he would simply waffle. I recalled the opinion of a male friend of mine who claims that when it comes to relationships men are less honest than women – and he is probably right! Of course there are some exceptions.

Of one thing I was certain. In the early years we were always open because we understood each other on such a deep level that we could be honest about everything. In 1955, however, there was a slight gear change, almost imperceptible, but I was aware of it.

I always knew that Odd could attract the opposite sex – like moths to a flame – but then I understood that because I was similarly blessed – or is the word 'afflicted'? Anyway, over those waiting years, of course we both had our dalliances, but we always told each other about them as they were unimportant compared with the beauty and strength of feeling we experienced together. When Odd met Sigrid, perhaps it started as a 'dalliance' but it grew into something much deeper. I can readily understand that he couldn't bring himself to tell me about it in a letter. He waited until he saw me again, in May 1955.

I was glad I had just resisted asking *why* he had left me. There are some questions better not asked. The past is the past after all – let it rest in peace. Anyway, what purpose would it serve if I told him now what a devastating effect our parting had had on my life. At the time, he knew that I forgave him, without reservation. Although I must admit that losing my man did impact enormously on all the relationships that followed, but I did not blame him for that. It is not what happens to you in life, it is how you handle it that counts and, back then, I was too immature to cope appropriately. It took me some five years to sort myself out, but in the end I emerged a much stronger person. Perhaps I had simply grown up – and for that I was grateful. Some people never do.

Anyway, enough of the past. What matters is the here-and-now, which I find absolutely delicious!

Oslo, February 3rd 1954

Dearest, dearest

I just got your letter – that lovely blue envelope – with your dear handwriting.

And I just got the surprise! THE SURPRISE of 1954. What a fantastic thought – what a wonder to happen in the middle of an ordinary day. How is it possible that a *dream* can stand the greyness of the daylight – be realised – put in the shape of *fact* – and yet be a beautiful, inspiring and soft *dream*?

What have I done to deserve this? I almost thought that happiness had left me – and now it smiles at me again.

You are marvellous, darling. First you are a perfect Tour Organiser having dug out Norway of all the cold and snow-covered countries in old Europe. That reveals a refined taste! Secondly – and in earnest – I admire you so much for the way you spent Xmas and especially New Year's Eve! That conveys to me much more than thousands of words. How I love you for that Marge! And your letters, how they have developed to pearls of beauty and expressiveness. Later I think I'll frame them!

Back to wonderful reality. You leave London Monday 8th and due in Geilo Wed 10th (I'll order perfect weather for your crossing – I know one of the chaps at the weather forecast unit!). I only regret I won't be able to stand on the pier at Bergen with the red carpet to welcome you. And another big regret – darling, you ask me if I can spend some time with you up there. I know I once suggested I would take a job as ski instructor, as I know that students from Oslo University have done that in the past. However, in order to balance my account, I have been obliged to take a teaching job *every night*. That is a very sad state of affairs but I am afraid I cannot leave Oslo.

Darling, is it possible for you to come to me in Oslo? I'll personally take care of the training in the wonderful skiing terrain we have right outside the door – and I'll be your humble servant day and night – except for the two hours every evening when I'm teaching (perhaps you could join me in one of my English classes, so please prepare a little lecture on Australia – or tell about your first meeting with the snow – or your first experience with skis on). I shall of course book a hotel for you and other necessary details.

I know it is pretty impertinent to suggest a thing like this after you have had all the trouble of coming to Norway, but is it possible do you think? Darling, please write and tell me as quickly as possible. Anyway, I will telephone you on Thursday February 11th at 2:00 p.m. I imagine you would be at the hotel at that time and I'll have the pleasure to hear your voice again and, hopefully, discuss how to meet and other beautiful aspects. This is not true – I can't believe it.

(Then there is again quite a lot about Bridie, which I'll skip.)

Marge, I feel like a child, so full of expectations. I only hope that our meeting will be another pearl of beauty that the *reality* cannot reduce. There is so much we have to talk about, darling. How I look forward to it, even if I know that not everything will be pleasant. I imagine long hours dragging mile-long coffee from a cold pot – and the vital feeling of a human contact beyond words. I feel the thrill of dancing with you, feeling the tenderness expressed in every movement of your body.

I dream – I dream, darling – and soon I will experience the dream. What is a week? It is a second compared with the usual dimensions of our waiting – yet at the same time it feels like a year.

Right now I am in the usual coffee house – I must bring you here one day and show you the historic table – I love it!

Darling, I must finish now, here is my new address…

How I miss you darling, and how I am yours – forever,
Odd

"When I arrived in Geilo, Odd, I found another letter from you waiting for me ."

Oslo, February 8th
My dear Marge

I hereby have the extreme pleasure to wish you welcome to old Norway! I could tear a telephone directory in pieces from anger and despair at not being able to be there on the spot – and not being able to kiss your mouth that must be so cold in the vicinity of the North Pole.

It is like a thousand and one nights to realise that, at this writing-moment, you are leaving Newcastle. I am sitting here in a lonely room – and perhaps you are staring eastwards across endless waves to Norway – and the wonderful future we have in front of us.

It is a wonderful thought, Marge, you in Norway again.

When I telephone Geilo, please be in, so we can plan our future paradise. I am missing you terribly and longing desperately to see you ... and hold you in my arms...

If you possibly can, leave the ski club and come down here to me (with your ski equipment!). I would love you even more if you come as soon as possible – what about departure Fri 12th?

'Til then I am counting the minutes, dearest Marge. All my love to you – and what a wonder to be able to say "au revoir".

Your longing Odd

"Of course I did leave Geilo as requested and travelled down to you in Oslo – do you remember, Odd, that week we spent together?"

"I do, Marge – or some of it anyway. The skiing in Nordmarka – and your tumbles in the snow. Poor you – and the night we spent in the cabin cuddled up in front of a roaring fire."

"Odd, I think I have some ciné film of our little cross-country skiing expedition. Of course I haven't seen it in over 50 years but I am certain I wouldn't have thrown it away – I didn't discard any of those precious mementos. As a matter of fact, I have one here amongst the letters – some words you wrote to me at the Hotel Viking."

"Ah, Marge, my dear, I do indeed remember the Viking."
"On a card we picked up in the restaurant, you wrote –

Your eyes
    Darling,
    they express my longing, my solitude,
    my sorrow, my despair
    and my hope and faith *too*
    Your presence darling is my life
    Alltid din, Odd"

"I think that's about all the emotion I can take for today, Marge."

Chapter 7

At the Radisson Blu Hotel Odd had booked us for a few nights. He thought it would give some variety to my stay in Trondheim. Besides, it was the opportunity to share a great big comfortable double-bed, instead of having to manage in the hospital bed his doctor had insisted on – or the sofa I was sleeping on.

Our arrival did not start well.

As we entered our room, Odd tripped and fell very heavily. The staff member who was showing us in was most concerned but Odd could not bear any fuss. However, he did accept the offer of drinks 'on the house' – so down we went to the bar to help recovery!

That evening we decided to give dinner a miss and instead have a liquid meal in bed. We had brought a bottle of champagne with us and lots of nibbles so it was fun to just chill and enjoy the bubbles – and lots of conversation about how our lives had been over the years. We also discussed poetry, and especially his poems.

"I am sure, Odd, that your essence must shine through in your poetry. I deeply regret that I did not learn Norwegian when I had the opportunity, because now I would be able to appreciate your poems. I would love to understand – in particular – your last book which I am sure must radiate the sum total of everything life has thrown at you."

"I must translate some of them for you, Marge."

We then discussed our different experiences of running a school. Odd told me about all the work he had done on curriculum development and teaching methods, and about his trips to various countries to research new developments.

"Now that's enough about me. Tell me about some of your experiences, Marge. It was clear from your book that you have led a very full and exciting life with a great deal of travelling. Your work for that international federation took you all over the place. I was fascinated by your travels in the East, especially your trips to India. Fancy being invited to tea with the President of that remarkable country. V.I.P. status indeed! You have met so many people of significance. I enjoyed also learning about your administrative, financial and negotiating abilities – and your organisational skills in arranging so many big events really impressed me. When I read your book, Marge, I felt so proud of you."

"Thank you darling. I gather that you too have had an interesting life, and you seem to number the cream of Norway's artistic talent among your friends."

"Perhaps, but I repeat, it is *you* I want to hear about. Take me back to when you first arrived over this side of the world."

"Arriving in the U.K. in 1951 is indelibly imprinted in my memory. It was cold, wet and foggy. London was still licking its war wounds. Compared with sunny Australia, people looked pinched, struggling to get a grip on post-war life. Everything, it seemed, was in short supply. There was still rationing of course, which meant that dining in a restaurant was not a particularly enjoyable experience. I also recall ghastly breakfasts with scrambled, powdered eggs and endless baked beans. We made London our headquarters for our European travels and I remember that everything on the other side of the Channel seemed to us more cheerful, more recovered from the scars of war. But to return to that first day in the U.K. We booked into the Cumberland Hotel at Marble Arch, unpacked and got ready for dinner. This was our first night in London, so I decided to wear my brand new, chic grey suit.

Seated at our table in the hotel's restaurant, Mother ordered roast something-or-other. I was so excited, I didn't have much appetite: a salad was all I felt I could manage. When the waiter approached our table he was carrying our two plates and balancing a huge bowl of mayonnaise on Mother's roast potatoes. Unfortunately, just as he drew near, he tripped, the bowl of mayonnaise went up in the air and landed squarely on my head, upside down of course! There was mayonnaise everywhere. What a welcome to London I thought – but I could not stop laughing. All Mother could say was 'Oh, your beautiful suit.' In minutes the restaurant manager was at our table offering profuse apologies. He asked me to go upstairs to my room, get out of my clothes and the Housekeeper would collect them from me. Everything, he assured me, would be cleaned and pressed overnight. At 8:00 a.m. sharp my clothing was returned, not a speck of mayonnaise to be seen.

We were offered dinner on the house the next night, but we

declined. We decided instead to try a restaurant in Soho and that too was memorable for a different reason. We were just about to order when in flounced a rather grand looking woman, somewhat eccentrically dressed, who was clutching a white poodle in her arms, adorned – for his night out – in a diamanté collar and a coat resembling a tuxedo. Back home dogs were never allowed in restaurants. To our amazement this one was not only allowed in, he was given a chair at the table and his owner tied a napkin around his neck whilst he consumed a similar meal to the one she was having. The English are so good at eccentricity.

Remembering this little happening reminds me of another amusing dining experience which happened onboard ship on the way over. Amongst the passengers were two sheep farmers, brothers, who were making their first trip abroad, which was also their first time on a big liner and, before boarding in Port Melbourne, they had had their first shopping expedition in a city. They each bought three-piece suits and hats which they wore non-stop throughout the entire three and a half week voyage. Whether they were seated around the swimming pool or attending the Captain's cocktail party, the garb was the same.

It was understandable of course. They had spent their entire lives on a vast sheep station far from the niceties of city life. As an example, one evening in the restaurant (their table was right next to ours) they ordered asparagus as a starter. When the waiter served it, he gave each of them a finger bowl. Dave said to Ron 'Hey, what the hell is this for?' Ron replied 'Don't be so bloody ignorant' – and with that he removed his false teeth and rinsed them in his finger bowl! Unbelievable, but true. I wonder what happened to them. I do hope they enjoyed their trip to Europe.

Returning to those first days in London, there was something we both wanted to do which we could not do in Australia and that was to go into a pub and put our foot on the rail. Licensing laws in Australia back then were strict – 6 o'clock closing, no women allowed in the bar, only in what they called 'the ladies' lounge.'

We were fortunate in having a letter of introduction from someone in Melbourne to a friend of his who was not only a Londoner but, as well, a recently retired Scotland Yard man. When we met up, we got along really well with him and he certainly showed us many aspects of London that were not on guided tours – including of course many visits to pubs. He took us to the Old Bailey to watch a trial, to one of the few remaining old Music Halls, to the House of Commons to watch MPs in full flood and to the East End to give us a glimpse of the more seamy side of London life. We must have walked miles with him over a long and very interesting weekend.

Is that enough for tonight, Odd?"

"No, I want more. Tell me, did you ever have any *dangerous* moments in your life?"

"Oh my God, yes, loads of them. Where do I start?

One really frightening episode happened when I was travelling with Mother. It was on our way back to Australia, so it was after I had met you, but I don't think I ever wrote to you about it because it was such a long and complicated story, and we never really understood what it was all about. I'll try to summarize. We crossed the Atlantic by ship and during the voyage we met a man, in his early forties, who was very attentive, especially to me. Towards the end of the voyage, he told my Mother that he had enjoyed meeting us and that he wanted to see her daughter again. Would she have any objections if he paid us a visit in Melbourne within the next few weeks? He had business interests in the UK and Canada and was interested in exploring possibilities in Australia.

That evening my Mother was wearing a fur jacket. He remarked on the quality of it and said he knew a lot about furs because an old friend of his was one of Canada's top furriers. Just by way of making conversation, my Mother said that she wanted to buy me a mink stole – the height of fashion in the 1950s. The fact that I did not want one, nor anything else made of fur, did not deter her for a single minute, bless her. He offered to introduce us to his furrier friend but Mother explained that we had great difficulty getting enough dollars for our trip through the USA and Canada, due to the currency restrictions of that era, and she did not have anywhere near enough with her for such a big purchase. He said this was not a problem, he would gladly pay for it and Mother could pay him back when he came out to Australia. In private I told Mother I would not wear it, to which she replied, "Then I will." She adored furs.

As planned, we went off for two weeks to the States, then it was on to Toronto for a few days before joining the Canadian Pacific Railway for the journey through the Rockies. As his business was in Toronto, we agreed to meet him there. He entertained us lavishly and showed us the sights – ending with a visit to the furrier. It is very rare for me to dislike someone on sight but I did not take to the furrier at all, and his two male assistants were equally scary.

The mink stole was to be delivered the next day and our new

friend was to come to our hotel, at the same time, with the money in cash. The next morning, as I was unsure of the time of our appointment, I rang the hotel where our friend was staying and was astonished to be told that he had booked out the night before – and, no, he had not left any message for me! In a panic, I rang the furrier to tell him what had happened. To say he was displeased would be to put it mildly. He pointed out that it was a special order, they had worked well into the night to complete it, even my name had been embroidered into the lining. I apologised again and explained that we had not yet exchanged addresses so I had no way of contacting him but suggested that, as an old friend, no doubt he knew his address – and could pursue the matter if he so wished. "He's not a friend, I only met him a few hours before he brought you to my salon."

It was getting stranger by the minute! It was time to pack, as we were due to take the train that evening. Later in the afternoon, there was a message that someone was waiting for me at Reception. To my surprise, it was the furrier's two scary assistants. They approached me from either side, rather menacingly with hands deep in their overcoat pockets, and said (I shall never forget the words), "Come on, babe, we're going for a ride." It was unbelievable, a scene straight out of a gangster movie!

At that precise moment, thank goodness, a huge crowd surged in through the front door of the hotel, returning from some big – and boozy – sporting event. I allowed myself to be swept up by the boisterous crowd, all clamouring to get in the lifts. In the general mêlée, I got away from the furrier's two henchmen and melted into the crowd which backed me into one of the lifts, leaving them behind. Upstairs I quickly told Mother the story and together we barricaded ourselves in our room, pushing the dressing table and chest against the door – then rang for help. In minutes, the Manager, Assistant Manager and House Detective arrived and we told them our weird story. After much discussion, their view was that it was an attempted kidnap. Did we want to get the police involved? No, we said, we just wanted to catch our train and get out of Toronto as quickly as possible. Four burly members of staff escorted us to the station, made sure we got safely onto our train and then stood guard until the train left. Obviously they took the incident as seriously as we did."

"What an extraordinary story, Marge. I should have been there to protect you."

"Indeed, you should" I said, "but to continue with my adventures. In my late twenties, I had a boyfriend who despite many fine qualities had an uncontrollable temper. Eventually, I had enough of his mood swings and told him I wanted to end our relationship. In his rage and frustration, he grabbed me by the throat and tried to choke me. I thought it was the end but suddenly he seemed to realise what he was doing and stopped. His remorse was almost tangible, he never stopped apologising, sending me flowers, writing letters, and promising he would change. However, I decided to move on. Interestingly, he died some 10 years later. He left me a legacy – and a beautiful letter.

As if that wasn't enough, in the same year, another man threatened to kill me. He was a business acquaintance I had lunched with a few times. One night there was a knock on my door and there he stood, clearly very drunk and brandishing a gun.

He told me his wife had just left him and he needed company. "All women are rubbish," he shouted, "but I intend to have you tonight – and if you resist, I'm going to shoot you!" I tried to shut the door but he pushed his way in, staggered then tripped, fell to the floor and passed out. I managed to get help from a neighbour. When he came round we plied him with strong black coffee, poured him into a taxi and sent him home.

There are many more narrow squeaks, if you want to hear them."

"Oh I do, Marge, I do. This is better than the movies."

"Perhaps a preamble is necessary before I tell you the next horror story. This happened in 1956 as far as I can remember. Anyway it was quite a while after we parted. I was about to start a new position and felt I needed a short break away, before beginning what promised to be a hectic and demanding new job.

I took myself off to Greece. Whilst there I had a horrible experience. I was raped by a Greek opera singer in Athens. He was twice my age and three times my size – but I must say he did have a wonderful voice! Foolishly I flirted with him, never thinking that it would lead to something so scary. I never reported it because I was too embarrassed and couldn't bear the thought of the fuss. I returned home by the first available flight, feeling rather worse than when I left."

"My poor, dear girl – how awful for you."

"There's more, but all rather different episodes. When I was married to Tom, we were in two car accidents in France on two consecutive days. The first one was in Fleurie where we had been staying with the Marples. He was Minister of Transport in the

93

UK, at the time. He also had vineyards and properties in France including a magnificent château. His plan was to turn it into a Health Home specialising in osteopathic treatment – and this was how we became involved. Anyway, we were travelling on the Route Nationale when a car, coming in the opposite direction, began to overtake at high speed. The Marples' car was hit on the side, spinning us round. We finished up with the front wheels over an embankment. Nobody was hurt but we were badly shaken. Then, the very next day, we were collected by a French friend with whom we were going to attend a conference in the South of France. On the Autoroute he suddenly discovered that his brakes no longer worked. Fortunately there was quite a wide grass verge, which he managed to get onto and we came to a halt in some bushes. Apart from bruises we were all in one piece, but again rather shaken.

Then, when I was married to Robert, we were in three hotel fires, all within a few months. The last one was the worst because it started in our room whilst we were downstairs about to have dinner – and both of us had given up smoking by that time! The cause, it turned out, was when the chambermaid came in to turn down the bed, a splendid antique four-poster, she switched on the bedside lamps and she must have knocked the voile bed drapes over the lamp so that, in time, the heat on the flimsy material set it alight and the fire spread rapidly.

I cannot really call the next one a dangerous episode because I didn't go ahead with it, but it *might* have been! I was introduced to an Arab businessman who was visiting London. When he returned to Lebanon with his English girlfriend, who was a friend of mine, he wrote offering me a job with his company looking after the press and public relations side of his business. Fares, accommodation, expenses would all be taken care of and the salary was overwhelmingly generous – was I really worth that much? Then over the next couple of weeks of corresponding, I discovered that what the Arab gentleman was really interested in was – a *ménage-à-trois* – the job was almost an optional extra! Thanks – but no thanks – was my reply.

You must be thinking by now that I am some kind of disaster magnet – perhaps I am. Anyway, this is the last 'near thing' for tonight – and it is actually a fairly recent happening.

I was holidaying with friends in Sicily. It was night, and we were in a dimly-lit part of the town. We were about to cross the road, when two men on a motorbike (Mafia, I'm sure) snatched the handbag from my shoulder. He held on to it – but so did I. As I was pulled along, he accelerated, which made the bag's strap break. I was catapulted into the air, flipped over and then I hit the middle of the road with a tremendous bang. I was stunned but, as if from afar, I could hear my friend's voice telling me urgently to move. I opened my eyes and saw two cars coming straight at me. With no thought for her own safety, my friend ran into the centre of the road, frantically waving to stop the cars from running over me. I escaped with nothing more than a small lump on my knee – and, most importantly – I still had my handbag! When we returned home, my friends gave a Sicilian dinner party and everyone was asked to dress Mafia-style. I must show you the photographs some time. We all look as if we are on the set of "The Godfather". It was such a fun evening and my friends seemed pleased that I had lived to tell the tale."

"I am surprised you didn't break a few bones, at the very least."

"I think your Marge must be quite a tough cookie."

"And yet so feminine!" he said.

"Now, I think it's time for some sleep."

Chapter 8

The following morning I was woken by the sun invading our room and through the window I could see an opulent pink and gold sky promising a sunny day. I was encircled by Odd's arms and I wriggled to wake him up.

"Time to get up, sleepy head."

He blinked. "It's so cosy snuggled here with you Marge" he said, as he nuzzled my neck.

"True, but I have a huge thirst. Must be that champagne-and-nibbles supper we had last night."

Downstairs at breakfast, we met a delightful American couple who told us they were in Trondheim for their daughter's marriage to a Norwegian. They told us about the plans for the wedding, and all the trips they had enjoyed whilst in beautiful Norway. Then they asked us what our story was. It must have been obvious that we were not an 'average' couple in their golden years, sitting there so close together and holding hands. We gave them a brief version of our story and they seemed very moved by it. After an hour or so of chatting, we parted company.

Odd and I went out onto the terrace to enjoy the morning sun and a cigarette. A couple of hours later, the husband of the American couple came looking for us.

"We haven't stopped talking about you," he said. "This is our e-mail address. Do let us know how you get on."

There is no doubt that everybody loves a love story.

We began talking about our families. Odd had been close to his Mother but had had a difficult relationship with his Father, who had rather despaired of his son ever completing his university studies. Life had provided quite a few 'hiccups', which inevitably slowed things down.

Odd had known my Mother, of course, and they were quite fond of each other. However, it must be said that he did pose a 'danger' so far as she was concerned. She lived in fear that one day her daughter might be lost to Norway.

"You had a complicated relationship with your Mother, didn't you?"

"Yes, I did. I loved her dearly and we got along really well together but, with the passage of time, I found the possessiveness very hard to deal with. She desperately wanted me to return to Australia and even went so far, on one occasion, to buy me a return ticket and leave it on my pillow – without any discussion! Then another time, she found my private journal, in which I recorded my thoughts and feelings, and to my dismay I found that she had crossed through, with a thick black pen, everything with which she did not agree! Could I not even think my own thoughts anymore?

It was like the last straw, and it made me all the more determined to stay on in Europe."

"I'm glad you did, Marge – and I do so admire your independent streak, which you have always had. Now, I think it is time for us to go back to our room and read some more letters."

"After my skiing experience in Norway, you may recall that I decided to have another go in Austria, as a girl pal of mine was keen to try skiing and she persuaded me to join her. You wrote to me in St Anton."

Oslo, March 2nd 1954
My love

Finally, I have been investigating the postbox many times a day even if I knew it was too early. Just now I arrived home – and it was there – significantly resting on the table with all its secrets and emotional content – a modern nerve.

I made a little ceremony out of it. I changed into my smoking jacket, slippers and all, had coffee – and sank into dreams and beauty! How I loved it! Your expressions, your thoughts, your digressions, your feelings. All! It was so much *you* that at last I could close my eyes – the letter faded away and I sank through a grey room of time and at the other side I saw *you* take shape and form and colour. You were sitting in a lounge somewhere in Austria. I *saw* you. You had been skiing, and now you were talking to somebody. But behind the words, I saw your longing too – and there was pain in your heart – as it is in mine – but you played your part well and did not reveal to anybody what mattered. I was content just to listen and look at you.

This is what I dreamt…

As always, the process of realisation seems to be slow with us. I went out into the new day – without you – it was snowing. The sky was white and empty and the branches of the trees were black prayers – silent and sincere. Suddenly I was attacked by an agony of *sadness* so sweet and so strong that tears came into my eyes. It was strange! It was not depression – it was just a philosophical sadness. I was painfully happy because of the beautiful moments we had shared recently. It was like a religious feeling. I felt strong.

I took off my hat and I sang a little melody to the white emptiness! Can you imagine? I felt as if my life was more straightened out. I thought of our conversations and our very honest confessions – and I realised that I understood myself better after this – thanks to you and your beloved faith. And I talked to you – "What does it matter if we are separated – when we KNOW that we are one?"

It was an elevated moment, Marge, and I shall not forget it.

Sunday I spent with Bridie – and I had dinner in 'our' coffee place, The Pavillion. I was not depressed either! For you were with me – that is the positive effect you have had upon me darling. I feel much more sure. Now, when the depression comes, I will let our moments of beauty parade by: the coffee hours on the roof of Oslo, the Viking night, the Humla one, Frognerseteren with a burning fire inside and in front of us, the night in the Students' Hut, your attacks on innocent Norwegians on your track! The hotel room with its beauty and ecstasy.

Darling, it was all beautiful – just like champagne. We continue to grow upon each other – and the contact seems to be similar to the contact between twins. I was not at all surprised when I found that you responded to almost any stimuli from my part. It was like a silent agreement – and the language, the 'background' and all the rest – were no obstacles – on the contrary!

Darling, I want to kiss you right now. Yes even *those* moments seemed to be uniform, didn't they!

Back to your letter. I am very sorry indeed to hear about the death of Roy – of whom you have told me sufficient to realise that it must be a terrible loss for your dear Mother – and I fully understand your desire to be at her side in this moment. What are you going to do if she asks you to return?

You must be having an awful time, my love. How I wish I could be with you. What can I do for you darling except to tell you endlessly that I miss you terribly, that I have faith in *us*, that I need you!

Enjoy your stay in Austria – I will write again soon.

Your longing, Odd

P.S. *Jeg elsker deg!*
Remember me to your girlfriend – and ask her from me to guard you against those bloody Austrians!

"We seemed to have been quite fond of each other, Marge."

"Yes, Odd, one could say that – in your next letter, a week or so later, you wrote of feeling restless. You had been offered a tour with a party of South Africans in April which you were tempted to accept, as it would have meant starting and finishing in London and therefore some stolen time together. But, you had finally turned it down in order to concentrate on the Bridie thesis. However, the letter did contain something very interesting. You had told me you were thinking about changing your name and you had asked how I felt about it. 'Fine,' I replied, 'if that is what you want.' We had discussed the possibility of living together in London (even Australia) and so I thought, mistakenly, that you wanted to change your first name – for obvious reasons. How wrong I was! In your letter you said: 'Do you know that in future the Encyclopaedia Britannica will have to list me under I. My name is now Odd F Irtun (not Irge, which I also applied for). So what do you think Mrs Irtun?'

(If I hadn't known otherwise, I might have thought that was a proposal!)

In your next letter, you said:

"I am sorry to hear you were disappointed with your prospective name – Irtun. I fully agree with your thoughts – and if you like I will forward a complaint to the Royal Department that was silly enough not to accept the charming abstract name, Irge. It feels strange to change names in the middle of life – as if one was changing one's personality. I am afraid I still can't get completely rid of my old one.

Dearest, this morning you were here again – in my room

102

and in my heart. Thank you darling for the expressionistic cards from St Anton and your letter from London.

I am very worried about the new situation regarding the state of your Mother. It must be difficult for you, obliged as you are to make a decision – 'Shall I give more consideration to her than to myself?' I suppose you were right in suggesting the idea that you would return if she wanted it. If that will be the case, it will be awful for us. But I suppose we are able to stand anything, as long as we KNOW that we belong to each other. However, the question is how would you be able to face your home and 'old background'? Before long perhaps you would become acclimatised and your European (and Norwegian) experience would become part of a vague and remote dream. Anyhow as an experiment the idea is awfully painful – but interesting. I am eagerly awaiting further news from you.

As for me and my little existence, sometimes I feel as if I were quite alone in this damned universe. There is so much hunger in me for the *love of you* that I feel like a prisoner in jail.

I have not heard from Mildred for weeks. I wrote and told her that I might go to London in April – and if not then, in May/June. I got an answer in which she strongly objected to it. I wrote back and put my foot down. Hence – silence. I have invited her down here for Easter as I told you – but have not heard anything. Probably she cannot leave the baby so early – but let me not bother you with my troubles.

I had an extraordinary experience today. In the lunchroom at the University, I entered into conversation with a charming young man just by chance. He told me he was going to Geilo for Easter and by intuition it struck me that this must be Vidar, the man you told me you had met. Diplomatically, I found out – yes it was! We had a cosy chat and parted like old friends. He sends his regards. The world is small, microscopic, isn't it!

Darling it is midnight and I am trying to get some sleep. Why are you not here right now? I am always yours, Odd

"Quite a long time after we parted, Odd, I received a letter from Vidar. As you remarked, the world is very small. He had heard that our relationship was over and he said he was planning to visit London and asked if he could call on me.

Over time things developed and to cut a long story short we became engaged. He started decorating the flat we were to live in, in Oslo, and his family began to make arrangements for the wedding. Back in London I was in a panic. How did I let myself get into this situation I kept asking over and over in my head – and it wasn't the first time I had become engaged – and then ended the relationship. In fact I repeated that foolishness a shameful number of times."

"Why, Marge, did you do that?"

"I guess I had lost my faith in love. As I could no longer feel deeply, when it came to it I couldn't commit either. Psychologically I was a bit of a mess and I went wild for a few years."

But to get back to Vidar, he was a lovely guy – sincere,

thoughtful, loving. I was fond of him – and the sex was good too! But there is a world of difference between 'having sex' and 'making love', two entirely different activities, and I realised finally that I was not in love with him. He deserved far better than I would have been able to give him – and so I called it off!"

"You know, Marge, it is such a joy that we are able to be so open and honest with each other."

"Yes," I replied, "and that's the way it always was."

"True," he said, "nothing has changed."

As it seemed to be confession time, Odd then told me that not long after Sigrid died, when he was struggling with grief, he heard from a former student of his, a much younger woman, in her fifties. From the sound of things she had always been attracted to him and, understandably, she now seized the opportunity and 'offered herself'. Apparently it went on for quite a while but ended with a lot of bad feeling on both sides. "Still," he said with that naughty grin of his, "the sex helped a lot at the time."

"Life is endlessly fascinating isn't it, such a tangled web? Of one thing I am certain, the world needs more people of compassion who are aware of human weaknesses but who do not judge their fellow human beings. More understanding and forgiveness would make the world a better place. If there is one thing I cannot tolerate, it's intolerance! Seriously though, I dislike hearing people criticize each other, because at times we are all rubbish – and at others quite angelic and capable of such great acts. I guess what really matters is being able to learn from one's mistakes. Life should be a constant learning process, always growing towards the light. Here endeth my sermon for today!"

Odd clapped. "What a wise girl my Marge is. By the way was that the end of the Vidar story?"

"No, not quite. He contacted me again, some years later, when I was married to Tom. We met for a coffee. He told me that he did marry eventually but it hadn't worked out and so ended in divorce."

It was time to go for a walk and take in some of the sights that Trondheim had on offer. Being centrally placed at the Radisson Blu, we enjoyed wandering around the city and meeting up with some of Odd's friends. One day, we met up with Håkon Bleken, Odd's oldest friend (and Norway's foremost artist). I was able to enjoy some of his amazing paintings that are on display at the hotel where we met for coffee. What an enormous talent he has!

It was time now to pack our case and return to the flat. As I packed, I told Odd how much I loved his clothes – great taste, great style – and in tune with his way of being, suitably youthful too.

Chapter 9

It was beginning to feel as if we had never been apart. We poured over our memories, examining the letters like the precious jewels they were, comparing our recollections of events. Rekindling memories is a strange business, indeed, meeting again after such an eternity was surreal. Re-reading the letters brought all those strong feelings we had for each other into sharp focus, as if they had been frozen in time – and now there was a thaw! Odd had said he was "awakened". For myself? Well, I think I had buried my feelings alive, so to speak. I wrapped them up with the letters in that ridiculous parcel with all the Sellotape, and then hid it at the bottom of the old pine trunk – forever, or so I thought.

It was strange to be in a domestic setting with Odd in his flat – cooking together, washing up, putting the rubbish out, etc – such simple things, but we had never done them together. In our twenties, the time we spent in each other's company was usually in hotels or students' accommodation, or public places like bars and restaurants – although he did spend some time with me in my Kensington bed-sit. But domesticity was not high on our agenda!

"I have just realised that next year, 2011, it will be 60 years since we first met."

"Yes, you are right, Marge. How shall we celebrate our anniversary? What about a holiday in Italy? I remember promising, many years ago, that we would take a trip there together one day. If my state of health allows it, we'll do that and, as we both love train-travel, let's go by train."

"Wonderful! There are so many advantages to train-travel – no long airport waits, no sea-sickness, no seatbelts, freedom of movement – and the scenery is immediate and non-stop."

"Yet another thing about which we agree, Marge. Now how about a letter or two?"

Dearest Marge

What a lovely girl you are – the postman is carrying his little heart out! First the four Bridie books and today the letter with the photos. Darling, you must never think you send too many photos – ALL are longed for and appreciated. But I can't see how the Austrian ski instructor's intimate gestures can possibly be fitted into a training programme – on skis, I mean! It is apparently impossible to leave you alone for a moment!

And how are you now? Studying hard? Can you manage to make up the lost time? Any news from home? Do you send me a little thought occasionally – and a bit of longing?

Marge, I am so often thinking about our brilliant

moments together. They seem almost unreal and so short, and yet so near, real and VITAL. Our minds seem so alike. Everything seems so perfect between us. I suppose I have said this before many times. Yet it is the conclusion I always arrive at when I enjoy passing through the past memories of our meetings.

Always yours, Odd

"The next few letters are long and contain several pages about James Bridie and how you were planning your thesis – and our various discussions regarding his plays – so I won't read those. Incidentally, I did so enjoy helping you with that project. I think it showed that we could work very well together on literary matters, as well!"

Dearest Marge

I have just come in after a whole day in Nordmarka Studentby Ha og Frognerseteren. It was a strange feeling to sit in front of the fire – alone – to listen to the guitar – to walk among the silent trees that whispered wordlessly – we know what you feel! And our dear waiter at Frognerseteren served me coffee and seemed to ask: where is Marge? The charming foreigner you brought here last time?

The sky was pink when I went home and I had the same *strong* feeling as I had the day you left me. There was Spring around me and I formulated beautiful sentences to you and wished you were with me to hear them because I know they would have pleased you. It was a lovely dream.

I am so eager to know if you have had any letter from home.

Regarding your Geilo friends, Gunnar and Vidar, who send greetings to you, I must tell you that Gunnar (who is *the* expert on women) gave you a very high degree of praise – a statement I am quite prepared to endorse! By the way, Gunnar invited me to spend Easter at a sports cabin somewhere in the mountains with a group of Geilo friends – but I have refused. I am going to spend Easter here in Oslo – alone – working on Bridie. Mildred took ill recently and so she will not be coming down here. Probably she will come in May.

It is 12 o'clock and I must go to bed. Darling would you like to join me? Probably there would not be any sleep – I miss you and I am with you.

Yours, Odd

P.S. I am enclosing my heart and my love.

Probably I will not be able to come to London until about June 1st.

Oslo, May 4th 1954
Darling

Have you been waiting? As if I don't know the answer – we are both waiting – always. But I have not felt like writing somehow – one of those moods again.

My dissatisfaction has been due, partly, to economic difficulties which have forced me to teach much more than I should – leaving little time to work on my thesis.

Next, I have had a 'fight' with Mildred who, by letter after a month's silence, has laid her veto against my trip to England. Of course she knows you are there – and it is not necessary to tell her I am going to see you. She understands that with every fibre of her being. She threatens to stop me and I only wish she would! It would give me a chance to bring things to a head.

I don't know how things will develop. Of course this incident has upset me – in addition to the eternal dilemma and I have been in a hell of a mood. The restlessness has brought me into a situation where, in order to forget, I have spent too much time in restaurants and hectic parties, where once I did what I should not have done – against *you*. You understand, do you? I mean it is *you* I would not want to hurt. Anyway I have started to regain the balance and am working again. Today I was encouraged considerably by receiving a little scholarship from my Professor to help finance my work on Bridie. Dear chap!

How I want your presence, Marge! It is midnight and strange feelings spark their message of longing to you.

I am here – and always

Your Odd

P.S. I have greetings to you from the members of my English class, whom you charmed on your last Oslo visit – also from Torry and Agnes – and Marvin. They all get a funny look on their faces when our names are mentioned together!

"Odd, there may be a letter missing. The next one refers to my visit to Oslo. If my memory serves me well, I think the tour you hoped to get, which would have brought you to London around June 1st, fell through and the next was not until August. Being the spontaneous creature that I am, I seem to recall that I decided I simply couldn't wait that long, booked a ticket and arrived in Oslo unannounced! I have some mementos from that summer visit to you in Oslo – a paper serviette on which you wrote, "I think we would be very happy together" – and on the back of a restaurant bill you wrote, "I am glad you came – I need you! Words, words how can they express my feelings at 11.45 p.m., June 15th 1954. My heart is in your hands. Your Odd." And there are photos too of our hiking trips, the picnic by the lake and the coffee house visits.

Oslo, June 17th 1954
Dearest Marge

Oslo is empty and ugly without you.

It was the saddest departure I have experienced – not in a violent sort of way but more in a philosophical way. It gradually dawned upon me that you were *leaving* and that I would be alone for two months. I felt as if the ocean swept over me and I lived still – but there was nobody to talk to, nobody to share oneself with. I could see you to the last second, your quiet movements as quiet as your way of being – and I shared your thoughts.

I have loved your presence in Oslo Marge – and we'll be clever and make the best out of our situation while these next two months pass by. I must also tell you that I am proud of you. My Marge. Be a good girl.

With all my love

Yours longingly, Odd

P.S. I have got a strong mind to start studying – and plenty of energy after our holiday together – so I'll give Bridie a real treat! Hope you will be able to concentrate too.

"Although we don't have any of my letters to read, in that package with yours were some pages in my handwriting, expressing some of the thoughts I had at the time. They make interesting reading:

'It is midnight on June 1st 1954 – and Odd is *not* here as we had hoped.

How long is it going to continue like this?

Have I got the patience?

This waiting, waiting is driving me crazy.

When will this situation be resolved?

Will it ever be resolved?

The other evening at my philosophy class, I fell into conversation with a very interesting man, a visiting lecturer. He invited me to join him for supper after the class – but I declined, giving some lame excuse. Why? I think I refused because I was quite attracted to him – and I don't want any involvement of any kind right now. A bit of harmless flirting is fine but nothing more. My life is complicated enough.

Oh, my Odd, I miss you so much – your company, your love, your physical presence. I need reassuring. I need a hug. I want your arms around me right now and I need to hear your voice telling me it will all come right one day soon.

We agreed our lives must go on during this 'waiting period' – but how many years is it going to take?

You really messed up big time in early 1953 – and now we are both – no ALL – paying the price. I must not forget Mildred, she too is suffering, poor girl. Even if she engineered events in order to get the man she wanted (surely one of the oldest female tricks in the book) nevertheless I still feel sorry for her.

You and I both love the theatre. Your thesis is about a dramatist. I hope to God you are not actually enjoying the drama of this whole situation? No, of course, you're not. What a monstrous thought. It's just that I am feeling desperate tonight – there is something about the early hours of the morning that seems to provoke strange notions.

'Patience, patience – keep calm' my inner voice pleads. The Australian Aboriginals have a word – DADIRRI – for that inner listening – and I was being told to 'keep believing, don't give up hope.'

I don't give a damn about marriage, it is being together that matters. That is all I care about.'

And that is where my scribbles ended.

"An interesting text, Marge. The last bit comes as a surprise to me. I always thought you really wanted marriage."

"No, not at all – for me it was a kind of optional extra. Absolutely great if both parties wanted it, but not essential. What counted for me was the relationship, the depth of the love and understanding, not all the trappings of the wedding. Given that we are talking about the 1950s, I guess I was rather ahead of my time in the way I viewed things then. Come to think of it, I was always a bit of a rebel."

" You know, Marge, I didn't marry Sigrid until 1958, which was three years after we broke up – and then it was actually her Mother (a very strong personality) who pushed for it. I remember her saying 'If you don't marry her, someone else will' – and so I did"

"After your first bad experience of marriage, it wouldn't have been surprising if it had put you off ever doing it again."

"Perhaps you have a point. It is a beautiful day now, Marge. It seems a pity to miss the sunshine." At this point, we had a visit from the lovely four-legged resident of the garden. I don't think Odd had ever had any pets and he seemed almost surprised at how fond he had become of this cat. "How about the three of us partake of some sunbathing in the garden? I'll get the sun loungers and I suggest, Marge, that you get us a couple of nice gin and tonics."

For two or three hours, we soaked up the sun, held hands and went on reminiscing.

"Tell me some more about your trips to India. I don't want to hear about how beautiful the Taj Mahal is, I know that. Instead I'd like to hear your reactions to places and people. I seem to recall that you stayed mainly with families rather than in hotels."

"Yes, that's right. We had many contacts in India and wherever we went we were invited to stay with people, which made the Indian experience so vital and meaningful. They have a saying: 'our guests are our gods' which illustrates how hospitable they are, no matter how humble – or grand – the home. With such a variety of contacts we were taken to places that we would never have seen as tourists. For me the most memorable experience was our tour of the Buddhist sites which brought all of my previous reading of Buddhist books into sharp focus. I picked some leaves from the Bodhi tree, which I put in an envelope, and I have carried that little package in my wallet ever since."

"It was under the Bodhi tree where Buddha attained Enlightenment wasn't it, Marge?"

"Yes, that is the belief – and there has been a Bodhi tree on that same site ever since. Another unforgettable experience was going on a small boat along the Ganges at sunrise. On the banks of the river we saw many funeral pyres being set alight. It was interesting too to see those who chose to sit cross-legged at the edge of the river deep in meditation – and so many of them were Westerners. A visit to India is such a spiritual experience, on so many levels – if you are open to it. Of course you have to be able to cope with the poverty and the beggars as well, which is deeply distressing – especially in Calcutta. I don't know what the figure is today, probably much less, but then we were told there were over a million people living on the streets in Calcutta – and they maim their children too, so they can become more effective beggars. On one occasion we were in a taxi, it was a very hot day and we had the windows down. The taxi came to a stop (to let a sacred white cow cross the street) and a woman thrust her head inside as close to me as she could get in order to beg – and she had only half a face! It was such a shock; obviously she was a leper, poor woman. We had a doctor friend who took us to a leprosy centre. It was heartbreaking to see what that dreadful disease does to the human body. He took us as well to an interesting hospital on four floors with each devoted to a different medical approach – orthodox, homeopathic, ayurvedic and naturopathic. Cleanliness and hygiene were not high on their list of priorities – but then that is the way things are in India, which reminds me of another story.

In Calcutta we stayed with a man with whom we had corresponded for several years. He was a millionaire who supported Nature Cure activities, which was how we got to know him. In India, natural therapies are inherent to the Indian tradition and an intrinsic part of village life, with their close association with Ghandian ideals. Anyway, his house was in fact a high block of flats in the middle of the city. He had sons and daughters plus their families living on each floor, with the 'Guest Suite' on the top floor, which sounds rather grand, but it wasn't! He was a Jain and that particular religious sect does not believe in any outward show of wealth. The extravagantly named Guest Suite was a double bed with the greyist sheets I have ever seen (I preferred to sleep on the floor) and the so-called bathroom was running water and a bucket. Throwing a bucket of cold water over oneself was quite invigorating in a hot climate. However they were such a warm, welcoming family, and the meals – eaten as always cross-legged on the floor – were absolutely delicious. In the middle of a curry one evening, our host presented me with a large block of Cadbury's chocolate. He was so pleased with himself for having acquired it. Actually, he was quite an unusual character, the only man I have ever met who carried photographs of himself in his wallet wearing nothing but the briefest briefs, and in various poses to show off his muscles. Obviously he went in for body building and was rather proud of the result. It was when he showed me the photos for the third time that I began to worry about his motives; any moment, I thought, he might produce a copy of the Kama Sutra – but he didn't. The day we left, I discovered why the sheets on our bed were so grey. The servants were sent up to prepare the room for the next guest. To our dismay they did not change the sheets, instead they swept the bed with a dirty, well worn-broom!

Everywhere we went we were greeted with a garland of flowers. The day we spent with the Ghandian Peace Foundation visiting villages and hearing about their work and ideals, I finished up with so many garlands around my neck I could hardly see over the top!

Then there was our stay in a Nature Cure Home in Gorakhpur. Our room there was also memorable, for rather different reasons. There was a big centrally placed bed which was encased in mosquito netting. On a raised platform opposite the bed was the loo which was actually just a hole in the floor. During our interesting stay there, observing all the treatments, we both developed Delhi Belly, as diarrhoea is called in India. Although the stomach pains were agonising, there were some funny moments when, in the middle of the night, we were both trying to disentangle ourselves from the mosquito netting to see who could get to the hole in the floor first.

Two other cameos, and that must be the end of my Indian reminiscences for today. We were determined to try and drink the customary red wine with our evening meal, but that was asking the impossible in most of the places where we ate. However, there was one exception where they did make an effort. It was a smallish restaurant on the outskirts of Delhi. The waiter conveyed our request for a bottle of red wine to the owner who scurried away looking worried. Some 10 minutes later he arrived at our table with a triumphant grin on his face. A very dirty yellow plastic bucket, full of ice, holding a bottle of red wine was placed before us with a flourish. We forced it down; iced vinegar could not have tasted worse – but we did appreciate their attempt to satisfy our request.

Another dining memory: I was invited to lunch by an Indian gentleman. It was a pleasant little restaurant and of course I ordered curried something or other. To my surprise he ordered fish and chips – with Heinz Tomato Ketchup. He told me it was the best thing the British gave to India!

"I loved every minute of your stories, Marge."

My return flight was booked for the following day but I think we were both in denial. Finally, we got around to acknowledging the fact that I would soon be leaving.

"So what do we do next, Marge?"

"I suggest more of the same."

"How about if I make a visit to you in Kent? I have a hospital appointment in a fortnight and after that I will book a flight for, say, about the end of July – for a month's visit, would that be alright for you?"

"Perfick," I replied.

I reflected that for once we were simultaneously single and could please ourselves what we did – and when.

We agreed to leave all the rest of the letters until Odd's visit to me. Instead, we decided on my last day in Trondheim to write a poem together. Odd pointed out that when we were in our twenties, we always thought – and talked about – the future, *our* future. Over half a century later, we think only of the NOW and we reminisce about the past.

"There is a poem in there and we must let it see the light of day," he said and continued, "Without thinking, tell me quickly what you think we have been doing during the past couple of weeks, Marge."

"Stimulating the mind, nourishing the soul and pleasuring the body. What a lovely combination of activities!"

"Indeed," Odd muttered. "I must give you copies of my other books of poems."

In "*Kjaerlighets Krefter*" (meaning The Forces of Love), he wrote – "Thank you for our very special moments together, everlasting. And in "Spor" (meaning Tracks) he wrote "We have followed our tracks to the beginning, the 1950s. Nothing has changed!"

I had taken a packet of photographs to show Odd 'The Old House' and garden – he seemed to like what he saw. Included in the packet was a copy of the booklet, that son, Nick, had helped me produce, with all the tributes to my Robert that had been made at the Celebration of his Life. One day during my stay, I saw him reading it – especially my contribution. "It must have been very difficult for you, Marge, nursing Robert for seven years."

"It was. Losing someone you love to dementia is unbelievably painful, the slow disintegration on all levels, first mentally then physically – and there's no cure. All you can do is be there for them."

"It was like losing seven years of your own life, Marge."

"No, that's not the way I looked at it. I nursed him because I wanted to, I wouldn't have had it any other way."

"Nevertheless, Marge, you have had more than enough. I do not want you to be involved with my illness. It has so many ugly aspects."

"Stop worrying," I said. "I am involved with you now. We can't put your illness in a separate box. Whatever happens, happens. We'll cope."

We were both quiet for a while, trying to push away unwanted thoughts. Odd broke the silence. "There was something I intended to do while you were here – make a film, a DVD, which you could look back on. Time has gone so quickly, but I'll fetch the camera right now and we can make a little start today – and then continue when I am with you in Kent."

On my return flight, I ran through all the wonderful days we had just spent together. I also told myself that there would be no more cigarettes until we were together again. I felt sure I could manage it.

For no reason in particular, I thought of the souvenir I bought in Trondheim on the morning of the day Odd came back into my life, the day he came to see me on the ship. It was a hand-painted china egg – and I had no idea why I bought it. It was only now as I sat ruminating that it occurred to me what a powerful symbol the egg was – of something new about to happen – a birth or rebirth, a new beginning. How extraordinary! Then thinking back to that letter from Odd about changing his name, another penny suddenly dropped! Of course, he wanted to distance himself from the wife and child he didn't want – and what better way than by changing his name! Why did I never think of that before – I suppose it was because I was so fixated on the idea – quite wrongly – that it was his first name he wanted to change.

Mulling over names caused yet another penny to drop

– amazing how long it can take sometimes! Growing up in Australia, I was always called 'Marge' (Australians are notorious for shortening names – and words) and this label continued into adult life and throughout my marriage to Tom. However, when our marriage unravelled and I subsequently moved in with Robert, I decided this was the perfect moment – new beginnings and all that – to announce to everyone that my name was Margery and that was what I wanted to be called henceforth. (A few friends and family members have never quite managed to accept the small gear change.)

What I now realised is that it was something much deeper that precipitated my pronouncement about my name: I have always loved the way Odd said my name. The timbre of his voice and the touch of accent made 'Marge' feel like a warm embrace. If that was something I couldn't hear any more (little did I know that 'Fate' had other ideas) then nobody was allowed to call me 'Marge' anymore. It had to be Margery.

On arrival back in the UK, in a somewhat euphoric state, I was met at Gatwick by friends who said immediately how different I looked. Not surprising – I felt as if there had been an enormous increase in my feel-good hormone. I was rejuvenated and it struck me that I was probably glowing like a visitor from out of space!

Chapter 10

I promised I would ring the moment I got home, which I did, and we talked for some 45 minutes. One wouldn't have thought that we had just spent all that time together!

During the weeks that followed, we spoke on the phone every single day – and sometimes several times a day. If I happened to be out when he rang, I would find such lovely messages on my answering service. Sometimes quite short like 'I just want to hear your voice, Marge. Ring me when you can.'

or 'I miss you'

or 'Your man is waiting impatiently for you to call back'

(Your man, he said Oh my!)

or 'What I am looking forward to so much is to have your head on my shoulder again and to hold you very close.'

The result of the hospital appointment was neither good nor bad – a plateau had been reached. But then, most unfortunately, Odd had a bad fall at home in his flat. He told me it had taken him a couple of hours to get himself up off the floor – and the pain in his back was excruciating. Odd's medical history beggared belief. Apart from the stomach cancer, he had undergone major surgery on his spine – *twice* – as well as heart surgery and, some years back, a stroke and … it just went on and on. And yet, during my stay with him in Trondheim, I never thought of him as being a 'sick' man, let alone an 'old' man. Indeed, far from it! He was in excellent spirits the whole time I was there, always interesting, amusing and loving. In spite of the fact that he had lost a lot of weight, he looked well and seemed positive about the future – even if nobody could tell him how much time he had left.

However, I kept reminding him that this was how it was for everyone. Life is unpredictable – in an instant it can change. Who knows which comes first, tomorrow or the next life? His doctor prescribed morphine for the pain, along with all the other tablets and potions he was taking, but it was clear that his back problem was causing much distress and making life increasingly difficult. After much discussion, he agreed to see a dear friend of mine, during his visit to Kent, for an osteopathic assessment of his problem. Having been through so much trauma and surgery, it was difficult to know whether his body would be capable of responding to treatment, but it was certainly worth a try. Until he read my book, he knew nothing of osteopathic medicine but he was now eager to see if it could help him.

The day of his arrival dawned and I arranged for a taxi to take me to Gatwick, wait and bring us back. The flight was running an hour late so the taxi driver, John, invited me to join him for a coffee. He was such a nice fellow and we were soon deep in conversation. I found myself telling him how Odd and I had met up again and, like everyone else to whom the story was related, he was very touched by it – and there was clearly a resonance in his own life. On the return trip, the three of us chatted away non-stop and parted like old friends. Indeed, as he left, he enveloped us both in his arms and told us to make the most of every minute together. Needless to say, we had planned on doing just that!

My house dates from around 1645 and has bags of character. Odd loved it – and the garden – and soon settled in. We had never lived together and I found myself thinking, as I had done during my recent stay in Trondheim, that it was such a new experience to be sharing domesticity – whether it was food-shopping, making the bed or watching our knickers, socks and shirts whizz round together in the washing machine! I still could not believe it was happening.

We decided it was time to do our first entertaining 'as a couple'. I invited my osteopath friend, Simon, and his partner, Jane, to dinner. It seemed a good idea for them to meet socially before attending for treatment. It was a jolly evening, the first of quite a few during his stay and, as expected, they got along really well together.

Emerging from the treatment room after his first consultation, I was astonished to see Odd walking quite quickly, straight-backed and *carrying* his walking stick. "Frankly," he said, "I do not understand what he has done to me but I feel great – and no pain."

The following morning, which was sunshine perfection, Odd was sitting on the patio waiting for me to serve breakfast when I heard him declare, "Marge, I am in paradise, truly in paradise.

What a lucky boy, I am!"

It was wonderful to see him so relaxed and happy. "I think it must be time for some more letters," he said after breakfast.

"I'll skip the next one and start with the letter you wrote just after we had spent some days together in London. This was one written at sea on August 21ˢᵗ 1954."

My Marge

A picture of rolling waves right in front of me – and a sky resting on the sea, sun-edged clouds and the subdued murmur from the ship's heart.

And my heart full of all-knowing rest and the memories of pleasant hours together with my sister – and lover – my companion and my dream – *you*.

You are closer to me than ever. I see your warm eyes as I saw them in the moonshine in Stratford, full of honesty and positive, constructive love. A building love which I never felt before, that you gave me. And I saw the outlines of a new future, and my wish to *share* this with you becomes more and more conscious.

Even if I did not love you (what is love?) I would like to marry you on the basis of profound *respect*.

You have been with me all the time – so it does not hurt so much to have parted. But of course the heart is deserted – and feels like a tree in a storm.

Your stronger and better, Odd

"Odd," I said, "although that was a beautiful and loving letter, it contained a sentence which sent a chill through me. I remember my reaction so clearly. I would not have wanted anyone to marry me out of respect, profound or otherwise. What made you say that?"

He hesitated and then said, "I don't remember." What a rubbish answer, I thought to myself.

In late August 1954, I decided on a whim to go and live in Paris. My Mother had not asked me to return to Australia after all, but had decided instead that she would make another trip to the UK. I wasn't sure when exactly, so whilst I had a window of opportunity, it seemed like the ideal moment to sub-let my flatlet and take myself off to Paris. I had very little money left but felt sure – well, hopeful anyway – that I could teach English, and survive somehow.

"Your next letter was sent to me at the University Hotel in Paris, dated September 27th 1954."

Darling Marge

This is to certify that (1) with great enthusiasm I have collected three lovely letters and cards from my little blonde Parisienne (2) that a long letter from me is on the way to the paper (3) that a recently returned 'Tour Manager' has now settled down for the winter with an infinite longing for Paris in his heart (4) that the same Tour Manager is proud of his little Parisienne who (according to her own words) seems to escape systematically all French mischiefs and is even making progress in her French studies.

I hope you have had tolerance to excuse my long silence

but the tour has really been so hectic. And all the time I have missed you – and tried to imagine how we could have enjoyed Italy together. All the time – there was so much that could have been even more beautiful.

From Mildred, no letter as yet – after my one which I told you about. I am trying to find balance in my mind and develop ordinary habits. I believe I will manage it because I have a desire to penetrate the studies. Your persistence is a stimulating element to me!

I miss you Marge – and want you in *all* ways.

Your longing Odd

P.S. If things become too intolerable I'll come to you!

And then two days later, a long letter to Paris.

Oslo, Studentbyen, September 29th 1954

Dearest Marge

This is almost the same room as we shared last time you were here, and I can't help turning round every second to see if you are sitting on the sofa. Right now the sun, which has become a legend only up here, is warming the room and my neck, and I start wishing it was your arm, and your voice behind it.

But my Marge is now a Parisienne – and is warming the necks of the United Nations – not me!

The idea of coming to Paris which I played with is now a utopia. Instead I have an appointment with Mr Bridie who is waiting for me on the table. Actually I look forward to start working and I think I can manage a few months without taking pupils. Bless them. And by that time Mr Bridie will have enriched science with my thesis born in pain.

There is quite a good climate in our flat here – we are five students sharing.

By the way, I have proved to have a latent talent for cooking. For the past two days I have prepared my meals and they have tasted delicious. So you will have expert guidance from your husband when the time comes!

Let me tell you about Italy, Marge. We went by train directly to Rome for two nights then on to Capri for three nights. Bellissimo! The weather was 100% – the beach and the water profound, and I paddled in a canoe exploring green and yellow grottos, and flirting with chocolate brown nymphs. And the piazza! Full of exotic beings – full of freedom and essential atmosphere … exhibitionism – and above all an incredible moon. Narrow streets, friendly faces, and the sun everywhere. Axel Munthe's Villa – was just like a piece of music to me. No barriers for human thought there.

That is the first place we will go, next Venice, with a side trip to Florence. The Uffizi galleries should be visited once more. Then Assisi – that charming little medieval village associated with the founder of the Franciscan Order.

And Venice – imagine we two in a little boat off the Lido. Well, this must be enough – or I will go crazy by the mere thought of it all.

I hope to hear from you soon. How long are you staying

in Paris? And when do I see you next?

Still no news from Mildred.

I'll start looking around for a job for you – even if I know it will be a long time before you can come here. Any news from your Mother?

I hope you are alright and that you feel what I feel now – and always, Odd

Oslo, October 11th 1954

My dear Marge

Our lives have been reduced by another week – and what is different? That is a big question – and I can only answer that my heart is NOT different, behaving as it does always with youthful jumps when a letter arrives from you.

My congratulations on the success in your studies – clever girl, I am proud of you. And now you have only a short month left in Paris before returning to London to meet your Mother. The next time you go to Paris, it will be with me on our way to Capri!

I left you last Saturday with a card only. I had a wonderful trip in Nordmarka – the autumn colours were fantastic – and then the moonshine and stars in the evening when I arrived at the cabin ... imagine my thoughts on a night like that!

The rest of the week has had no sensations, just putting the finishing touches to the decoration of my room – and the result is not too bad. There is a definite atmosphere now with a Degas reproduction (the ballerina on the stage), one etching, two drawings and a painting by Inger Sitter, a young artist I know. Then there's my guitar which I use to frighten away guests, and a lamp with a white lampshade covered with hotel stickers from all over Europe, The Dorchester taking a prominent position (need I tell you why? I will do it anyhow: it was that night I had just arrived in London and I waited for you in my hotel room, so restless I could neither sit nor stand. And then THE MOMENT – the moment when you slipped into the room – and were mine again!)

You should have been with me today in Nordmarka. It was profound! Darling, I must stop now but I promise to let you hear from me again soon. In the meantime – be a good girl and miss me – just as much as I miss you.

Right now there is soft American swing music on the air, and I dance with you in my thoughts. Goodnight Marge

Love from

Your Odd

P.S. Have not heard anything yet from Mildred. The next step will be another letter from me and we must meet somewhere to talk things over.

"Stop letter-reading for a while and tell me about your adventures in Paris."

"It was a magical few months, I loved every minute of life in Paris. It is a beautiful city and it has such an intoxicating atmosphere. You will probably remember that I started off at a little hotel at the foot of Montmartre, as the couple who ran it were the only people I knew in the whole of France – and actually I had only met them once before. They advised me to go to the Left Bank and find some cheap student accommodation, enrol at the Alliance Française, which gave excellent language courses, and put a card on their notice board announcing that I gave English conversation classes. They explained that there were students from all over the world studying French at the Alliance and many of them would have some knowledge of English, therefore it was probable that some would welcome the opportunity of improving their conversation skills in English.

I followed their advice to the letter and it worked out very well indeed. I found a room in a student hotel near the Boulevard Saint Michel. It was basic to say the least but it was all I could afford. I had virtually run out of money, and had gone to Paris on a one way ticket, Newhaven – Dieppe, which was the cheapest route. The hotel was on six floors but there was only one bathroom – so it was necessary to book an appointment for one's once-a-week bath. For the days in between I became adept at my ablutions with the basin and the bidet in my room.

There was only one member of staff, apart from the Patron, and he was not quite all there in the head, poor lad. He was supposed to do the cleaning but he seemed to spend a lot of time looking through keyholes. I remember waking up one morning with the feeling I was being watched. My bed was opposite the door and suddenly I saw his eye peering at me. After that I left a jacket hanging permanently on the door handle. And then there was the loo – only one on each floor – and of the ghastly hole-in-the-floor design. The whole hotel smelt of gauloises, pee and camembert, if you can imagine that – but I loved every sordid detail. It was just so exciting to be living in Paris and there was a real villagey feel about the area where I lived. Everyone was so friendly.

For breakfast I used to go to the *boulangerie* right next door where they served big bowls of café au lait and hot croissants straight from the oven. Heaven! There were always lots of students in there and I soon became accustomed to the French habit of shaking hands the moment we met and then when anyone left, and if I bumped into one of them half an hour later we would shake hands all over again. As we all got to know each other better, the greeting became a kiss on each cheek. Interestingly, a French habit that over time crossed the Channel and is now more or less universal in England."

"You know Marge, when I think about you going off like that on one of your whims to a country where you didn't speak the language, didn't know anyone and didn't have any money, I think you were very brave."

"Foolhardy would be a better word, Odd."

"Well, you would know of course, but I still think you were brave. Please continue, I'm enjoying this."

"For lunch I would buy a baguette, a piece of cheese and a tomato and eat my humble fare on a bench in the park. I must have walked miles and miles every day exploring Paris, usually in the afternoons after my French classes and my English conversation students. Loving art as I do, I spent a lot of time visiting galleries too – which brings to mind an artist I met one day at an exhibition. She was an interesting woman of about 40, Russian-born but had lived in Paris most of her life. She invited me for drinks at her apartment so that I could see her work. Actually it was more a studio where she lived than a flat. It was crammed full of her paintings (some quite explicit female nude studies I noticed) and many – mostly erotic – objets d'art. She asked me if I would sit for her, she wanted to paint my torso – nude of course. She said my breasts were perfection. Oh my, she was clearly of a different sexual bent and she was trying to seduce me. I would rather have coped with male seduction any day than this predatory woman who was really scary. However I told her I was not interested in her advances and eventually I was able to extricate myself from her amorous overtures – and left feeling shaken – but not stirred!

In contrast to the frugal life I was leading, from time to time I would be fêted by an English or Australian friend who was passing through Paris. Fortunately I had taken one posh frock with me and so could rise to the occasion and enjoy being wined and dined at the Tour d'Argent or some other top restaurant. The next evening I would be eating at the student haunt where we could get – for practically nothing – a three course meal and a glass of wine. The portions were small, but adequate."

"So life in Paris suited my Marge very well, eh?"

"Indeed it did. I met so many fascinating people – and was often invited to their homes or flats, some of which I remember vividly. For example there was a flat on the Ile St. Louis to which I was invited for dinner. It was one large room with an adjacent area that was kitchen, lavatory and shower room all in one – no doors, no building regs to cramp one's architectural inventiveness, and definitely no health and safety issues to worry about.

Another apartment I recall was on the Left Bank. It belonged to an American I had met at the Alliance. He was a man in his 40s who had been married to a French woman, but now separated, and he was still trying to learn how to speak French. He could read a French newspaper but, because he had no ear at all for languages, when he endeavoured to have a conversation in French, nobody understood a word!

As my accent was quite good, I tried to help him with his pronounciation – and we became friends. Now, his flat was what might be termed shabby chic, decadent even. The thing I found amusing about it was the shared bathroom which had a door either side of the room. One had to remember to lock the appropriate door in order to avoid being disturbed. One day when I was there visiting my friend, I charged into the bathroom for a penny-spend and found a young (forgetful) man in the bath. He was totally unruffled by my intrusion and said 'Ah, bonjour, Mademoiselle' and offered his wet hand for the customary handshake. 'Bonjour Monsieur, je m'excuse' I replied, beating a hasty retreat.

That evening, my American friend introduced me to a French couple, a Count and Countess with whom he had been great friends for many years. The following weekend they invited us both to their Château outside Paris. It was full of wonderful paintings and antiques. What a contrast to where I was currently living I thought to myself, as I sipped champagne by the lake.

In spite of this occasional high-living, I had to face the fact that I was skint. On what I thought was my last day at the Alliance Française, I saw a card on the notice board to which I responded immediately. An American blouse manufacturer was in Paris on business and wanted the services of an English-speaking secretary for a few days. Perfect! I got the job and he paid me very handsomely, which allowed me to stay for a while longer in my beloved Paris. However I decided to ask the Patron if I could change my room. Apart from having been invaded by insects (fleas I think) during the past week, I was unhappy about the man who lived in the room next to mine. He was a medical student from Guadeloupe and he had started knocking on my wall during the night. Then he asked me to go dancing with him. I declined. He got angry and accused me of being racist. I have never been perturbed by anyone's race nor the colour of their skin, it was the look in this man's eyes that I did not like – he looked lustful and dangerous. He really frightened me so I moved up to the 6th floor – *sans ascenseur*! It was a claustrophobic room with a frantic wallpaper in black, brown, purple and orange but at least there were no knocks on my wall – and no fleas!"

"What would you say, Marge, was the highlight of that particular stay in Paris?"

"Without doubt, the 14th of July. What a festival of music, singing, dancing in the street, entertainment, fancy dress, exhibitionism. Everyone seemed hell-bent on letting their hair down and having fun – and of course we finished up in Les Halles for the traditional bowl of onion soup – a night to remember!"

"I think my letters will sound rather tame after all that French excitement."

"Let's finish with your last letter to Paris."

Oslo, October 14th (or is it another date?)
Dearest Marge

It is Sunday evening – and I have my weekly session with you, Marge. It is some sort of holy moment, and I almost feel awkward to express that I miss you (I think I will let that stay implicit for the future!). I am alone (naturally) but also in another sense. These last days I have felt rather unusual. 'Something' has filled me with fear. It is difficult to define but it has made me restless and almost dizzy. I do not know what it is. Perhaps the sign of a coming danger? It almost feels like that – and naturally I want to talk to you. That would help I am sure. I cannot describe it here – it refuses to be addressed in print. So let me change the subject.

Following my return I have met Marie who has just returned from London and Paris. She is living with a friend of hers (female), a painter. She has changed considerably – for the better. We have been to a couple of parties together – and it appeared she did not know about you and me. She thought everything was at its old status. I had to tell her about us. What we felt, and how things were. It was a shock to her. But she knows now – what she cannot understand is when I said: Marge made me honest, against myself as well as against everybody. But she is a marvellous girl – so she will not make any difficulties. But she is 'dangerous' because there are so many things that fit together between us – well, except that ONE feeling! That feeling that makes me shiver when I am with you. That feeling that makes one wonder about everything – thoughts, feelings, actions, ideals – the things you do that I want, and say – unexpectedly – that I like.

I am almost glad to hear that you have to leave Paris soon! It is beastly to hear how you turn the heads around every cosmopolitan shoulder. I am equally glad to hear that your French is improving (when you have time for it). Continue to take care of yourself.

Your Odd

Chapter 11

All our reminiscences had transported us back to our twenties – with the same playfulness, laughter and spontaneity. At times we were even a little crazy.

There were, however, a couple of days during his Kentish stay when he was not at all well. One day, in particular, we had to cancel meeting up with some friends because he could hardly get out of bed. Then I discovered why he was suddenly feeling so unwell, he had been taking twice the dose of morphine! His back problem was continuing to respond well to the treatment but I think he had suffered so much pain one way and another, over such a long period of time, that perhaps, even unconsciously, he had increased the morphine dose ' just to make sure'. Of course, he was disregarding completely the possible unpleasant and serious side effects. For the highly intelligent man that he was, he could be less than sensible about his health.

One day, Odd said to me, "I notice that you don't take any pills at all, Marge."

"You're right, absolutely nothing. Having spent most of my life in the world of natural therapeutics, I am well aware of its benefits – but I'm not fanatical. I think the key is balance – the Buddhists' Middle Way – and, of course, it helps enormously if one has good genes."

"You are a wonderful example, Marge, of the healthy lifestyle you have followed for the past 50 years. I have never seen anyone of your age with so much energy. It's impressive."

"Well, you know the saying, 'If I rest, I rust'."

Odd's friend, Marie, telephoned several times whilst he was staying with me. She was anxious to know how he was – and her calls brought the conversation round to something that was troubling him, indeed he had raised the matter in his letter back in May following his return from a stay with Marie in France. *"I have told her about you, and our rendezvous in Trondheim … if you and I get together (!) … the time I have left … what will happen to her?"*

"Odd, my darling man," I said. "You do not have to make a choice. You have known Marie since your university days – you value her friendship. I would not dream of asking you to cut yourself off from her – why should you? Let's face it, we are all in our eighties. For God's sake, any one of us could drop dead tomorrow, today even! There is no need for big decisions – and I include in that the question which I know you have also been pondering – should we two move in together, and if so, the UK or Norway? My suggestion is that, for the time being, we live in the NOW – and embrace every beautiful moment. Criss-crossing the North Sea is something we have done before, why not let history repeat itself? Come the winter, if you feel you want to miss the worst of Trondheim's weather by going to the South of France to stay with Marie, as you have done for the last few years, then by all means do so."

"Marge, if I did, how about if you come to France, as well? I think you and Marie would get along really well."

"If you are thinking what I think you are thinking, Odd Irtun, then stop thinking it. It would not work! Even for the most open-minded of people, there are limits!"

Later that day, a few friends popped in for drinks. With them was the cousin of my friend Odysseus, Greek-Cypriot concert-pianist Martino Tirimo. He and Odd hit it off immediately, discussing music and poetry and, of course, Cyprus. Odd had spent the winter in Cyprus every year for 10 years and had written many poems about it, as well as articles for Norwegian journals about its history, culture and politics.

We had been talking about translating some of his poems into English as I had an intense desire to understand them. "Let's start with the Cypriot poems," Odd suggested. We spent many happy hours in the garden working on the translations. Where I could help was suggesting alternative words or phrases to fine-tune the English. We also read poetry to each other. I have quite a collection of poetry books in English and French. It was such a lovely pastime.

Music was another passion we shared and here again our tastes were so similar. I had bought myself a copy of the CD "Secret Garden" that Odd had introduced me to in Trondheim. It was composed by a Norwegian, Rolf Løvland, and performed in conjunction with the famed Irish violinist – Fionnuala Sherry. It had become 'ours' and one day we sat clasping hands across the dining table listening to "Secret Garden" with the whole of our being. I felt tears silently trickle down my cheeks and his eyes too were full of tears. It expressed so perfectly our emotional landscape – without words. It felt like the pinnacle of pinnacles, the ultimate of ultimates, a spiritual orgasm. The intensity of being so in tune with each other is something that will live with me forever.

It was time for more letters – extracts only.

Oslo, November 21st 1954
My dear Marge

A couple of days before I heard from you I had finally a letter from Mildred. I had been expecting her to arrive for the past week. As I understand it there were different reasons why she could not come – partly she had been sick, partly the short time before Xmas etc … Now she expected me to go home in order to enjoy the Holy Christmas with me, and later, after the holidays, she would go with me to Oslo. My Mother, who had visited her recently, told her that I was coming home.

My reaction to the letter was that more than ever I realised how my life has been tied up to people and things that want to force me along lines I do not *want* to follow. Some call it responsibility. I call it a prison. And I want freedom. The dilemma that has troubled me every day has been:

Shall I go home to Narvik this Christmas – follow the line, doing what is expected of me, have a 'nice time' in the family lap, and then take her to Oslo – and tell her that I can't go any further. *Or –*

Not go home, but tell her right now (what she must know – as I have told her many times already) that I must get my freedom before I wither completely. Do the thing by correspondence, then wait and see. However, that would be very humiliating for her and the family on both sides.

I have not been able to make up my mind until today. And now it is clear to me. I cannot go back and do the same absurd playacting again, listen to all the enquiries and the planning for a life I cannot take part in with my heart. I cannot go back and sacrifice my own identity, my own self. My whole system objects. I cannot.

So what I am going to do is write her a letter saying that I cannot go back – without any explanations. This as a sort of compromise because I do not feel like destroying her Christmas completely. After Christmas she can come down here or not, I don't care. In other words I shall not express clearly, before Christmas, that I want a divorce – but very indirectly, and almost as effectively.

Marge, does this sound complicated and unreasonable? I feel I must operate with points of time, instead of being frank and saying at once what I want. This is part of my policy to pay consideration to her – which now has come to its bitter end.

I feel much better now I have a line to follow, and now *we* can face the future with greater optimism.

It must be hell for you in London – waiting, waiting. But now, Marge, something will happen very soon! It helps me to know that you have that beautiful faith in me and in us and the future. I need it, and I love to hear you express it. That same faith is growing bigger and bigger within me, Marge. I think often of the many things we have in front of us. All the things we shall make come alive with our conscious way of living – for we must have learnt something from all of this! We shall touch everything with our magic stick – and make it feel alive – just like we do...

After all what does it matter that we are separated now when we know that we exist and that we are going towards the same end?

You must not lose your faith, but instead prepare yourself for our next meeting – all the things we shall experience, discuss and solve together. I do not know but lately I have started to dream so intensely about these things, in a lyrical way, which I hope we shall be able to live up to.

The picture which now enters my mind when thinking of you is the moment when you were sitting in the Grill Room at the Dorchester – I believe it was my birthday – I approached the table, you were really there, blond with a knowing smile, and a heart full of expectations of the small things, a look, a touch of the hand – and our big secret which we shared without words.

If my finances would allow it, I would not hesitate to go to England this Christmas, as it is going to be pretty bad here in Oslo. But that is impossible unfortunately. How will you be spending it? I think I will go up to one of the distant sports cabins in Nordmarka and stay there among the trees in the snow. I have always felt like doing that and now I have the chance – to be all alone in the forest, with the incredible silence around you – and eternity within you.

Now darling I shall finish, hoping this letter finds you in good health and that it will induce you to copy my fecundity! And very soon too!

Marge, here I place all my love and longing

Yours, Odd

"Enough letters for today. Whilst you were reading, Marge, I have been observing your paintings here in the drawing room. I remember you said there was a story behind every piece of art you had – just the same applies at home in my flat, as you will recall. Yet another thing we have in common."

"Gets boring doesn't it" I teased.

"Never", he replied with a twinkle.

"Returning to the paintings, yes indeed, either they were done by artist friends or bought somewhere special as a memento, like that piece of jade I bought in China with some money my darling step-daughter had given to me."

After a look around, Odd asked me if I had ever tried my hand at painting.

"Yes, as a matter of fact I have – and I loved it, although my talent is rather meagre. Would you like to see some of my efforts?"

"Indeed, I would."

At the end of the viewing, Odd picked out two which he asked if he could have. "You should take it up again, Marge and develop your talent, particularly as you enjoyed it so much."

"Yes, I do intend to at some point. When I was nursing Robert, it was July 24th, and the Doctor advised me to take a break for just a couple of hours a week and do something creative and all-absorbing. I arranged for a carer to take over one morning a week – and I followed various courses – flower-arranging, art, pottery. It was good advice and I think it saved my sanity."

"Now, over our evening aperitif, I would like you to tell me about your very first sexual experience. Knowing what a memory you have, Marge, I'm sure you remember it."

"Indeed I do – and it still makes me laugh. I was just five years old and my best friend was the little boy who lived next door. We used to play together every day and we got along really well – *most* of the time.

This particular day we were in my garden making mud pies. Suddenly, he threw one at me, for no reason, making an awful mess of the brand-new dress I was wearing. I was *very* cross.

The opportunity to retaliate soon presented itself. He needed to go to the loo. We had a rarely-used outside lavatory in the garden. It was a huge old Victorian affair with a wall-to-wall heavy wooden seat and the hole was so large it had the potential to engulf small child-sized bottoms.

Well, I waited until he had been in there for a minute, then I pushed the door, which opened inwards, pushing him further down into the hole so that he got stuck and then I left him there!

Eventually my Mother heard his screams for help. We were both scolded for our respective acts of naughtiness – but that was not the end of the story.

Usually, in the late afternoon, we were in the habit of having

146

a chat through a hole in the fence bordering our two houses. He was still very angry with me and, unable to think how to express it, he decided suddenly to thrust a certain part of the male anatomy through the hole in the fence. It was a shock and I thought it was very rude.

Guess what I did to get my own back."

"I can't imagine, Marge, tell me."

"I bit it, *very* hard!"

"Ouch, you naughty girl! Well, you certainly started young. Perhaps that explains why you are so good at…"

"Stop right there. I think we need some soothing music to elevate the tone of this conversation."

"No, please Marge, continue, I am enjoying this topic. Do you have any other funny, sexy stories?"

"Let me think."

I began to giggle.

"Yes, there is one that springs to mind. It happened in Paris. It was just after everything was over between us – and I was in a couldn't-care-less rather dangerous frame-of-mind.

You will recall that I was eking out an existence in that wonderful city by giving English conversation lessons. One of my pupils was an Iraqi who was studying at the Sorbonne. I suspected he was a perennial student as he had been living in Paris for many years and he must have been at least 30. One day he invited me to go dancing at a club he frequented. What a dancer he was! He was very slim and he had a way of holding me that made it easy to follow him no matter what the dance. He was quite a mover – and we danced the night away.

The next day he asked me to join him for supper, and he would cook. Kitchen facilities were modest to say the least in student accommodation on the Left Bank, but with inspired shopping and imaginative cooking, one could rustle up rather a good meal – and he did. However, it was his bed-sit that lives on in my memory. It was all red: red walls, red tinted light bulbs in the lamps, a red satin cover on the double bed with big red pillows. In the corner of the room was a screen across which walked camels in one of those bad taste desert scenes. Camels also appeared on the mats either side of the bed. Quite an Arabian Nights setting.

After dinner he whispered in my ear 'no woman can possibly imagine how amazing sex can be unless she has experienced an Arab lover.'

This full-on seduction scene made me want to laugh. I couldn't possibly take it seriously but I was in such a what-the-hell state of mind that I thought to myself 'OK, go for it girl – let's put his claim to the test.'

He then asked me to undress and wait for him on the bed (not in – ON he stressed). Meanwhile he disappeared behind the screen with the camels on it. When he emerged he was covered from head to toe in a sweet-smelling oil. He threw himself on top of me, and then I too was covered in the sweet-smelling oil. There seemed to be oil everywhere, and on the slippery satin bedcover, there was no way we could come to grips with each other. In the end we slithered off the bed and fell into an oily tangle on the floor.

I could not contain my mirth any longer. I laughed and laughed, but he didn't see the funny side. In fact he looked crest-fallen and rather hurt. My uncontrollable laughter was something of a passion-killer, as I could not but help notice that his ardour was diminished.

Now, enough of these sexy stories. I'm going to get our minds on a higher plain with some classical music. I feel as if I've been in the confessional – what does my priest think?"

"You have absolution my lovely girl."

Chapter 12

When I opened my eyes, the first thing I saw was Robert's portrait on the bookcase next to my bed. Did I detect disapproval in his eyes? No, I think it was my own sense of guilt with which I had been struggling a bit ever since meeting up with Odd again. Would Robert have understood? It was six years since he died. Then I remembered a conversation we had in the Nursing Home just a few weeks before his death.

I had been with him all day and during the morning he could only utter gobbledegook but later in the day we had a meaningful conversation. Dementia is such a mysterious illness – away with the fairies one minute and making a lot of sense the next. One blessing – perhaps the only one in seven long years – was that he always knew me. On this particular day he said:

'darling there is something I have been wanting to ask you – are you courting?'

(Courting, such a sweet old fashioned word)

'No' I replied 'absolutely not, please put that thought out of your head. You are my one and only love.'

He smiled and said 'I'm so glad.' Then a moment later, he took my hand and said 'But remember life must go on.'

It was as if something had switched on in his brain just long enough to convey these thoughts. For the rest of the day, he lapsed back into his own little world of madness.

The morning sun was flooding into our room heralding a trip to Rye in Sussex with dear friends, Simon and Jane. But before they arrived to collect us, there was time for some more letters to accompany our morning coffee.

Oslo, December 1st 1954

Dearest Marge

What a lovely letter to get in the last month of the year. It means most to me that you shared the beauty of the play with me, that you went straight home and put down on paper what you felt after the Christopher Fry evening. What does it matter that you passed into happy dreams and did not continue the letter until the following Sunday? It is nice to read the diary of people who interest you and I must say that you interest me, darling! What I like is your searching for spiritual beauty and reality, and the fact that we find them – or try to find them – in the same things, is not only a tie (I hate the sound of that word) but a sea of love that kisses and connects our longing shores!

I have not seen the play yet, so will abstain from further comments. One point however I must make. You say, "The play is a heart-rending plea for *humanity* – all human life regardless of how base or unworthy it may be."

I fully agree. A play should deal with every aspect of life. Even the ugly things *should* be beautiful (I have difficulty to realise that in practice) because they all have a *function* in Life – which does not mean to say that things have to remain ugly and base. They should grow upwards to the light, to the beauty. I must admit I am coward enough to avoid ugliness, baseness and all that, because I find life is short and it is necessary to make an assortment of experiences. Well, this is one of my reactions to your remark.

I have just read your letter again – I don't know how many times – and it makes me happy! This is because you seem to be so strong, so independent – and all the other things I appreciate so much. Your remarks on our situation of being apart – and its usefulness – I am willing to endorse. We have a saying in Norwegian: *Ingenting er så galt – at det ikke er godt for noe* (Nothing is so bad – that it does not produce any good*)*.

"I am stopping your letter here as I want to talk about that Norwegian saying. I do so agree with it. In fact I experienced the truth of it when I was nursing Robert. On the one hand it was seven years of sheer hell – for both of us, although in different ways of course. I was determined that he would not make the hateful journey, through all the stages of dementia, alone. We were in it together and I had to remain strong and focus on the present. However, there was a positive side to all the suffering.

Being tested certainly makes you stronger and I think we both grew considerably. In spite of his dementia, Robert found reserves of strength that made him very brave. This in turn helped me to dig deeply and develop my inner strength. Buddhist teachings also helped me – as did clinging to one's sense of humour."

"Tell me how you managed that, Marge."

After a couple of moments I recalled a good example.

"Robert had many bad falls during his illness and in trying to save him I often got injured too. On one occasion he grabbed my hand as he was falling, and bent it back so far that my wrist broke in two places. So I was in plaster and my arm was in a sling. Robert asked for a cup of tea. I went to the kitchen and when I opened the tea caddy found there was only one teabag at the bottom of the caddy. I put my hand in and got it stuck. I asked Robert to pull it off for me but in his confused state he pushed it on with great force. Suddenly I saw the funny side of the situation, there I was with one hand in plaster and the other stuck in a tea caddy. I couldn't ring a friend, I couldn't get out the back door to scream for help, even if somebody called I couldn't open the front door – and all I could do was laugh. Robert joined in the laughter although I'm not sure he understood the problem. Eventually I put the tea caddy between my knees, gripped hard and pulled hard, finally releasing my hand.

What mattered most was that after all those years of frustration at his progressive inability to do even the simplest everyday things that we all take for granted, Robert finally achieved 'acceptance' of his situation, and in his last days he managed to convey to me that he'd found peace. For myself, the whole experience, heartbreaking though it was, taught me so much – not least, greatly-increased compassion, patience and understanding of human suffering. These are the reasons I resonate with that Norwegian saying.

We still have time for one more letter."

Oslo, December 23rd 1954

Dearest Marge

There are all the well-known Christmas tunes on the air – and I am trying hard not to be sentimental.

Only the wireless gives the life I want it to give. The books stare at me from the shelves. The work is lying in heaps in front of me, saying: here I am waiting for your energy. Get going! But there is a mysterious restlessness within me. A mind to do nothing. Just to enjoy the small things – and live.

I have just read your letter once more. Don't apologise for writing late. Always write when you feel like it. I know you are there anyhow! And I am glad you are in the same frame of mind. I enjoy hearing you regret that you make no progress with your studies. That kind of conscience is the root of all growth.

Marie has just rung to say she has left a present for me somewhere in town. She is on her way to take the train to Nötterøy to her family. There are twelve sisters and brothers and usually they have many guests at Christmas as well. Marie is, by the way, very much surrounded by a famous Spanish sculptor right now. He has an exhibition in Copenhagen and Oslo and insists with all his Spanish ardour that she should marry him. He has even asked his architect in Spain to start building a house for them – before Marie ever knew of his intentions. He has also made a fortune here by selling his statues that are truly very attractive. Anyway she has refused to share the Spanish sun with him.

I wonder what you will be doing on Xmas Eve? If you look out of your window in the evening you will see me in the skyline, in the darkness, and I will talk to you – without words. I will thank you for the all-too-few but beautiful moments we shared during 1954. That memorable year. That tragic – and that promising year. I will paint a huge question mark above the roofs of London – and it will have the colour of *hope*.

I have had a couple of nice festive occasions with Torry and Agnes lately. I will bring Marvin your greetings. I think I will spend the evening with him and his wife tomorrow. (It is touching how considerate people are when they learn you are staying alone Christmas Eve.) Even too many invitations, but just like you last year, I wanted to be alone. However on second thoughts it will be nice in the future to recall such an evening with Marvin. I think friendship is one of the most important things in life.

The day after, I will put on my skis and go into the whiteness and loneliness. It looks fine now, with a high winter sky, and just a little snow, sufficient to enjoy the year's first excursion. I certainly will look for you among the trees…

And what was Mildred's reaction to my letter? I was waiting and waiting. Then it came. It was a type of letter I had seen before. It was terrible. It was from her Mother –

somehow that woman fills me with fear. Well, Mildred was ill in bed – and she was wondering when I intended to stop disappointing her – and all that. There were threats too. She hoped this was the last disappointment, or what would be the next? Of course they understand, but it is this FRAME of family life they want to keep together. Once the frame is there, the picture is nice and harmonious. And everybody can enjoy it looking from – the outside.

Her letter scared me – I could not help it – but at the same time I was angry. Angry like Hell. And that led again to strength. I don't know whether Mildred had given her consent for her Mother to write. The first time, she wrote without asking. But it makes me absolutely furious to be dealt with by another person like this – in spite of the fact that she is the mother and very concerned about the health of Mildred which threatens to be worse every day. And she puts the blame on me!

I had better stop before I explode with anger and humiliation. And then there would be no letter for you – which perhaps would be better than receiving this one! Well, it looks like the New Year will have a dramatic start.

Before I close, I must tell you that yesterday when we had a visit to Rosekjelleren (that French-looking place in Oslo) we were 'entertained' by an exotic female dancer. And she had your hair, and your eyes, and was very like you! I was carried away completely – and my friends had to keep me back from the floor! (I hope it wasn't you?)

Now, this will be the last letter of this year – and that

fills me with melancholy which is enforced by that vast and hurricane-stricken *distance* between us.

Dear Margie, I miss you and hope the time is not too far away … the New Year we WILL make better!

Yours longingly, Odd

"It's time to collect our things together for our day out – cameras, sunglasses and jackets in case the weather changes."

"You think of everything, Marge. It's a new experience for me to be spoilt – and I like it!" It was a really lovely day, full of laughter and friendship.

The following day we went to Leeds Castle with Odysseus. Anna didn't join us as they had some Greek-Cypriot friends visiting. However, we went back to their house for tea which allowed Odd to meet some more friends from the island he loved so well.

When we got home it was still really hot so we sat in the garden.

"I have a feeling it is chilled white wine o'clock," Odd said.

"I have a lovely Sancerre awaiting us in the fridge – and I'll turn the fountain on as well – the sound of running water always makes the patio feel cooler."

"Marge, may I suggest you bring the CD player out here. I think we need some music – how about some opera?"

"Opera it is."

As we sat listening to 'La Bohème' I told Odd about my trip to Verona, some five years ago.

"Opera in the Arena is an unforgettable experience. For a start, it is vast. If my memory serves me well, I believe it holds some 20,000 people. There is no roof of course and it is more or less just as it was when it was built. The audience sits on stone steps – but cushions are available. If you half-close your eyes you can imagine the Christians being fed to the lions. When you first see it, it is quite breathtaking. I was in Verona for a week and I saw three operas. The last one coincided with Italy winning the World Cup – in the middle of the opera! Verona exploded as the win was announced. There was a deafening roar from the crowd outside which, of course, stopped the opera mid-aria. It turned out that many of the mainly-Italian audience had come prepared for this possibility, and brought with them bottles of champagne. Strangers were coming up and giving me a hug and thrusting a paper cup in my hand with warmish champagne – and this was happening all over the Arena. Some members of staff climbed up to the top of the wall framing the stage, waving large Italian flags. The national anthem was played to flashing lights of the flag's colours – and as for the noise outside, well, I think everyone with a car was tooting their horn. After an hour or so, they tried to resume the opera. Two members of the cast began to sing an aria – but it was hopeless, the noise made it impossible to hear them. They walked to the front of the stage, shrugged their shoulders and walked off.

Much later the opera continued and we left there about 2.30 a.m. – but did not return to our hotel. There was so much going on, on the streets of Verona, that we joined the revellers until about 4:00 a.m. What a blast – it was great fun."

"I love the way you relate your stories Marge, they are so vivid. I almost feel as if I had been with you in Verona."

"I wish you had been" I said. He gave me his irresistible smile and kissed my hand.

Chapter 13

I woke up to find him wrapped around me, rather like that lovely purple clematis of mine that entwines the branch of the apple tree.

"If you'll let me go for a few minutes, I'll go downstairs and put the kettle on. Would you like coffee in bed?"

"Yes please, I would. I find the service here at The Old House impeccable."

"We aim to please, sir. Of course, the Management hopes you'll make another booking."

"I will most certainly, in fact you might find it difficult to get rid of me."

"Perhaps – just perhaps – we won't want to."

With coffee finished, we planned our day starting with brunch in the pergola, for a change, at the top level of the garden.

Odd was going to be with me on his birthday – August 18th – unbelievably his 85th birthday! I decided to arrange a little surprise party for him. It was going to be tricky to keep it a secret, but I'd manage somehow. And what could I get him as a little present? I decided on a CD of Richard Burton reading poetry – and a book on Boxley written by our local historian. Next the guests. I didn't want to overwhelm him with too many people, so decided to invite only the friends he had spent some real time with during his stay – Simon and Jane, Anna and Odysseus, and Gisela, the German osteopath who was staying with me.

Apart from a walk around the village and a pint in the pub (happily right next door), we decided to have a day at home translating more of his poems into English, more filming, lots of music and some singing. Just being together was, well, Perfick Mrs Larkin.

"Can you cut hair, Marge?"

"Yes," I said. "I always used to cut Robert's hair and trim his beard."

We were in one of our zany playful moods so the haircut and shampoo turned into a full salon-type treatment! Facial, manicure, pedicure and full body massage. "I'm in paradise, what a lucky boy I am!"

Later in the day, we were discussing literature, drama, poetry and suddenly Odd said to me, "Marge, why don't you write *our* story – you could do it, I know. Your first book has shown you have a real talent for writing. I know you could infuse it with heart-swelling emotion – and some humour. *Everyone* who has heard about our meeting again and so on, has thought it was a beautiful love story – and you have all my letters you can use."

"Yes – I think I could do it. Anyway, I'll give it some serious thought, I promise – and speaking of letters, shall we continue?"

Oslo, January 8th 1955

Kjaere Marge

I don't mind a bit your "mechanical" writing. The cardinal point is the spirit behind the print – and you are certainly there all the time, with your short contrast remarks which a Bridie would envy you. Besides you type beautifully, and you will make an excellent secretary for me when I start writing my books and plays. Maybe you could take over the love scenes, whereas I could specialise in nature descriptions – and loneliness and frustration in every field. That is modern and greatly appreciated.

Didn't you see me on Xmas Eve? I was sitting on the wine glass and met you quite often that night – just there where I wanted to meet you. I was there again on New Year's Eve – on all the glasses – and I enjoyed your kisses.

Well, that was one part of me. The other had a white Christmas in Norway. In spite of firm resolutions to spend Christmas Eve alone, I had to yield to Marvin's persuading telephone calls and the night was celebrated with his wife and little daughter, without all the hysterical ceremonies. The night through we discussed yoga teaching, and he presented me with the old religious document "Bhagavad-Gita" which is the gospel of Hinduism. In time maybe you will find me an ardent adherent to oriental philosophy.

After many drinks and much talk, I awakened to a lovely illuminated morning, with an unborn sun just felt on the horizon where a rainbow of light was fastened above the distant hills. Late in the afternoon I started on my skiing expedition. It was already dark and my battery soon ran out leaving me alone in total stillness and darkness – among huge and serious trees that neglected my presence completely. I was not quite sure of the way in daylight – in darkness, even less. I had to use my Ronson to light the way and I just went on by instinct. It was dramatic and exciting – especially when I fell from quite a height that made my nose look like that of a sparring partner, and I received a very ungentle push from my rucksack in the back of my head (I thought I had discovered a new star). It took me six hours to find the place, fortunately I saw the lights in the distance. I was too late to get dinner but after a couple of øl I almost kicked the stars. It was a most unexpected crowd in the hotel. Mainly teenagers from Oslo trying to escape family tragedies, and they were all "greasing their trotters ecstatically on the beeswax".

It was quite nice after all – and the skiing conditions were excellent. I always associate the trees in Nordmarka with you after the trip we had together.

Well now, how are things in general? There has been silence for a long time but today I received a telephone call from my parents in Narvik (the first for a year). I learnt to my surprise that Mildred really had been ill. She had inflammation of the lungs. They had not told me about it.

I am going to take the next step.

It was awfully nice of your Mother to send me a personal note. I greatly appreciated it. Please let her know that! I hope the New Year will bring all of us the happiness we long for!

Have a great time on your travels with your Mother –
and write to your man in Norway because you know he is
always waiting for your words.

Yours longingly … Odd

Oslo, April 5th 1955
Dear Marge

Well, what happens here then? Mildred had written
and cabled the last fortnight announcing her arrival at
different times, but tonight at last it is going to happen.
She is going to take a job here for some time. And now it
is going to happen – it has to happen now, a short time
after her arrival this evening. I am not very happy about it.
On the whole it has been a dreadful few weeks. I have felt
so sad and miserable that little work has been done. The
tragic undertone is fortified by the slow arrival of Spring
and my intense longing for the mountains, the sun and
snow – I have never longed for it so much in my life. I wish
we could be up there together to be purified and get new
strength. I hope I do not depress you by my letter, but I have
to tell you this – the miserable state of my mind and soul.
Dear Marge, I want to leave everything and go with you
somewhere where there is solitude, and where nothing could
reach us. Nothing.

Of course in the immediate future I shall not be able
to be in contact with you but as soon as anything happens
I will write.

It is not too long now before I take off for London for

those two American tours. To sum up – there will be about 10 days in London in May and then 4-5 days in July. I know that is not very much – but let me know how this fits in with your plans and your Mother's travel projects.

I should love to talk to you right now – I really need it because in one hour the train arrives.

Dear Marge, I am with you, please do think of me!

Write soon

Odd

Oslo, May 3rd 1955

Dear Marge

I wonder what you have been thinking and feeling in this critical period of our lives? I am sure it has not been easy for you but you will, I know, understand my silence.

It took this long time to go through it, and I hope I can say it now, that I am through, that all is made clear, and the foundation of a new reality has been laid.

Need I tell you that it has been a terrible time? It sounds so easy when you are about to tell it, a series of facts, arguments and emotional outbursts. It is so easy the day after, but when you are right in the centre of the volcano, where everything has to explode around you, everything has to come up into the light of day, you feel pretty microscopic and helpless.

By God, it *is* over, after many weeks, she has agreed and she has left for Sweden where she has taken a job as she does not want to go home. I cannot tell all about it in this letter. You had better wait until I come to London, if you are

164

interested to hear the details. They are quite unimportant to you after all.

Now – I thought everything was over and settled and then I received another shock. The other day a letter from her arrived with bad news. It appeared she had lost her hand in a machine at the place where she is working. She did not have any money for lodging, food, etc and so she has asked for my assistance. I am trying hard to help and I do not feel too good about this new situation.

But this must be enough, I must not burden you more than necessary. I only hope that you will understand my unwillingness to write. I have not been able to do anything lately in my field – so please forgive me if the waiting has been too long. Thank you for your short letter in which you appear to understand me completely.

Now I am only waiting for my 'plane to take off and get away from here. Darling, it is not long now, and it will be extremely good to see you again.

Your Odd

"There are only a couple of letters left, Odd, but right now I *need* a drink. How about you?"

"Sounds good."

"Have you ever had a Pimms? It is the quintessential summertime drink in England."

"I have heard of it, but never tried one – do introduce me to yet another English delight."

I assembled the ingredients on the table in the garden. "A

measure of Pimms to three of lemonade. Add whatever fruits you fancy – I have sliced a ripe peach, some perfect strawberries and a slice of orange and lemon. Whatever the fruits, it is essential to add a sprig of mint and a slither of cucumber, lots of crushed ice, stir – and enjoy!" After the third Pimms, Odd was converted to yet another English pleasure!

Just then my friend and confidant, Tricia, called in to see us. She had heard all about Odd and was longing to meet him. We all chatted away for a couple of hours – and, let's say, I think they managed to charm one another!

After Tricia left we began to talk about friendships and how important they are in life. Odd said "It is clear you and Tricia have a lot in common."

"That's true and yet we are two very different people, but we share a similar sense of humour, a love of spontaneity and fun, a thirst for trying new things – and we are both fascinated by human behaviour. As you have just heard from Trish, she is a psychotherapist which is what I wanted to do, but life decided otherwise."

"I find it interesting that we probably come across differently to different people."

"That is for sure, Odd. I am certain my Buddhist friends consider me as 'serious' because I always want to talk about philosophy. Many of my osteopath friends probably see my serious side too, but to my Boxley friends I guess I come across as a fun-loving party girl."

"What a delectable mixture you are – and I am so glad you are back in my life."

"Me too."

The sun would soon be setting but it was such a balmy evening, we continued to chat in the garden.

"What attracted you to Buddhism, Marge?"

"I'm afraid there's not a short answer to that."

"No matter, we have time and I want to know everything about you. Start at the beginning."

"Well, from as far back as I can remember, I have always been drawn to all things Eastern. You have noticed no doubt all the Eastern influences in my home. I guess it started with my Dad's business trips to the East. In particular, I remember him talking about Java and Sumatra and I recall all the wonderful presents he brought back for my Mother – jade, silks, a Buddha, a wonderful brass incense burner, oriental vases and beautiful wooden carvings – superb craftsmanship.

I was brought up, of course, as a Christian. Although my family was not particularly religious, I was sent to Sunday School at the Presbyterian Church. One Sunday, when I was seven years old, I was told that I had to 'sign the pledge'. I had no idea what that meant but it was a pretty certificate (I have it still!) and so I did as I was told. When I went home and told my parents that I had been asked to declare that I would never drink alcohol, my Dad fell about laughing! I didn't have to go to Sunday School again after that.

I went to a very good school – a Church of England girls' grammar school. The Principal was an inspiring teacher. She took us for religious studies, which she called Divinity. For a while – a very short while – I almost thought I could be a missionary! Then the girls in my class all became communicants – but I opted out. I doubt if I could have explained why exactly. Perhaps a theistic religion did not sit comfortably with me even then. I wanted to discover meaning and purpose for myself, I didn't want to be told what to believe, I needed to explore. I am sure the reason I wanted to read Psychology at university was not just my fascination with human behaviour but a desire to understand myself at a fundamental level.

For a while, in my early teens, I used to go to our local Anglican church on Sundays, but it did not inspire me at all. At the end of the service, the congregation would gather together for a chat over a cup of tea, and what shocked me was that this pious group of people were so judgemental about their friends and neighbours, even the vicar came in for criticism! The conversation was full of gossip and, above all, very unkind. What had happened to tolerance, forgiveness, understanding and compassion? I stopped going to church.

Surprisingly, for a teenager, I used to think a lot about religion, philosophy and life's big questions. I must have had some kind of spiritual longing but I had no idea in which direction. Another thing that bothered me was the emphasis all the time on material values."

"Give me an example of what you mean, Marge."

"Well, for instance, if a girl became engaged, immediately all her friends would say, 'Let's look at your ring' – and the bigger the diamond, the more impressed they were! I could never understand this obsession with the ring, why not ask about the man, or their plans for the future? I suppose this was when diamonds, for

me, began to epitomise those things with which I felt uneasy a
nd disconnected.

No wonder I grew up without the usual female love of
diamonds. I could appreciate their beauty, of course, but never
wanted any. My Mother, on the other hand, adored diamonds –
and all precious stones, as did my sister. I suppose I was always
the odd one out in my family. No doubt my thinking was rather
undisciplined – but amidst the confusion, some kind of pattern
was slowly emerging. You'll be pleased to hear, my dear man, that
all this has been background information. I am about to answer
your question!"

"Oh, good," he said with a grin. "I have almost forgotten what
I asked."

"In the early 1950s, I bought a book on Buddhism – but never
got around to reading it. A few years after we parted, when I was
still in some kind of no man's land, a girl pal of mine, a really
good friend, sat me down and suggested I take a long hard look
at my life. She pointed out that I was flitting from one so-called
romance to another, like a bee in search of nectar. At the same
time, I was working hard and often very long hours. 'You need to
ease up,' she said. 'You are burning the candle at both ends – and
in the middle.' The following day, she gave me a book, Herman
Hesse's remarkable distillation of wisdom, "Siddhartha", based on
the life of the Buddha. I read it in one sitting and then reached
for the book "Buddhism" which had been sitting on my bookshelf
too long, unread. It was as if a bright light had been switched on.
This was what I had been searching for all this time. It resonated
with all my previous thinking and questioning. I don't think of

it as a religion, but more as a philosophical system. There is no blind faith called for and no dogmatic creeds. I like very much the need for self-reliance and self-exertion, the importance of seeing things as they really are and that truth has to be realised by oneself. Buddhism is not just something to be studied but to be lived, put into practice in one's daily life. I could go on for hours on this subject – but I think we need a break."

"Thank you dear Marge. I enjoyed that."

Chapter 14

Odd's birthday had arrived. I took a lot of trouble wrapping his present – in layers of sheer silver-grey fabric, tied with wired gilt-edged red ribbons.

"I have never received such a beautiful parcel," he exclaimed. "You are so artistic in everything you do but how did you know it was my birthday?"

"As I have told you before, I have been blessed with a really good memory." What I didn't tell him was that every single year I thought of him on his birthday. Perhaps it was because mine was also the 18th, just one month later – or perhaps it was just that the date … and the man … were so firmly etched in my memory.

We had a leisurely day and I persuaded him to have a longer than usual afternoon nap, from which I escaped, in order to prepare dinner, do the flowers, lay the table and, of course, make the cake.

I don't think he suspected anything so it was a genuine surprise when the guests arrived bearing gifts, the champagne corks popped and we had a very happy evening. At the end of dinner, when I brought in the brightly lit cake with two large number candles, Odd seemed quite overwhelmed.

"I haven't had a birthday cake since I was 10." After cutting the cake he made such a moving little speech about how wonderful it was in one's later years to make new friends, which he felt he had done during his stay in Kent.

Two days later it was Anna's birthday and we joined her for lunch at the Pepperbox, a lovely pub in the country, followed by a drive around some of the picturesque old Kentish villages, and all of us singing with the joy of it all.

That evening, I was in the kitchen preparing dinner when I heard Odd talking to Robert's portrait – of course he knew I could hear him.

"No need to worry about Marge, I'm taking care of her now. Sorry I never knew you, Robert – I like your eyes, handsome fellow."

"Yes," I said from the kitchen. "He was – and, you know, if I hadn't been in the equation and you had met up, I think you would have become firm friends as you would have had so much in common. I think I've remarked before that you two are so incredibly alike – not to look at – but in so many other ways. Come to think of it, that is not at all surprising. I'll let you ponder that remark while I lay the table."

"Tell me more about Robert."

"He had a great personality, a big heart and a delicious sense of humour. He was intelligent, widely-read, handsome, sexy, loving, flirtatious and sensitive.

(My God I could be describing Odd as well, I thought to myself.)

Robert also had a vulnerability about him, which stemmed from the emotional baggage he carried from both an unhappy childhood and his first marriage. He was a complex character, yet at the same time the most honest and open man I had ever met. I trusted him unreservedly. Having been a brilliant communicator all his life, it made his particular disease all the more distressing."

We had both had happy marriages, but there is no doubt that one's first big love is such a seminal thing. When we met I was young and no doubt impressionable. Odd provided a new and totally different horizon for my life.

He was the first man who had opened the door to my capacity for feeling. Teenage romances back in Australia had been all very well but this was an entirely different landscape. Suddenly I knew the depth to which I could feel – and the strength with which I could love. He was such a force in my life on so many different levels – and I knew that I too had been an important part of his life – indeed they were the very words he wrote in the front of his book of poems which he gave me on board the cruise ship.

When finally we parted in 1955, I clearly recall, amongst all the strong emotions, that feeling of 'unfinished business.' It was incredible that we had been given this second chance, this totally unexpected opportunity to retrace our steps, to rediscover each other – this time with the clarity and wisdom that two mature lives, well-lived, can bring.

With dinner over, I was jolted out of my musings by Odd's voice suggesting we curl up on the sofa together and listen to some music.

"Can there be anything more perfect than to listen to beautiful music with someone you love in your arms?" Odd asked.

"Perhaps the addition of two glasses and that superb bottle of Cognac you bought me would add another dimension to the perfection."

"You have such wonderful ideas, Marge – and don't forget *my* wonderful idea. I want you to write our story. I know you can do it."

"I'll think about it."

Time was slipping away. Odd was due to leave the next day. Anna and Odysseus had kindly offered to drive us to the airport.

"We have just two more letters to read, so shall we finish the job?"

"Yes, of course, but just remind me, Marge, where we got to."

"The last letter I read was dated Oslo, May 3rd 1955, the one in which you told me Mildred had finally agreed to divorce and she had gone off to a job in Sweden rather than return home. Then shortly after, you received a letter from her saying she had lost her hand in a machine at work and she was asking for your financial help."

"Oh, yes, well of course in time that turned out to be a gross exaggeration. She had only lost the tip of one finger – not her whole hand. It was just another ploy, I'm afraid."

I went upstairs to get the letters.

The next one was written some six weeks later – and much had happened meanwhile.

Odd had arrived in London mid-May and we had a week

together before he was due to play Tour Manager for a party of Americans 'doing' Europe. My Mother, rather diplomatically, had taken herself off to Holland to visit friends.

The moment he arrived, I sensed 'something' – of course we had not seen each other for nearly a year – but I had had a similar feeling when I received his last couple of letters – and because of the circumstances there had been fewer letters anyway. We went back to my flat – and made wild, passionate love. He was as ardent and tender as ever but – and it was a very big BUT – I felt he was troubled, distracted even.

At long last, he was able to find the words – and he told me he had met someone, her name was Sigrid, her family came from Iceland. He said he had first met her many months ago, introduced by a mutual friend, but then had not seen her again until fairly recently. (I wondered what 'fairly recently' actually meant.) He had not wanted to tell me any of this in a letter. He said that she was not well, she had some serious emotional problems (he didn't want to go into details) and he had been trying to help her; in the process, the relationship had developed. He was clearly very upset to have to tell me this but he wanted to be honest with me, even if he knew it would hurt. It was obvious his heart was in conflict. As for me, I felt numb, the world had stopped turning, my life was suddenly lustreless. He told me he didn't know where it was going; he was clearly in turmoil and could not sort his feelings out. I felt as confused as a child who had just been told Christmas was cancelled.

I had bought a record called "Ebb Tide" not knowing at the time that it would be played over and over again as it so fitted our mood – it was an incredibly sad piece of music, without words, it seemed to tell of loss and deep regret.

The rest of that week together was strangely beautiful. It was as if we had been on a long car journey together – and quite unexpectedly, we had run out of petrol – and neither of us knew what to do. We had had such an intense relationship over four years, and all of them crammed with difficulties, not least of which was separation. It was really quite strange, we had been so 'in love', it was almost as if we didn't know how not to be.

All of these thoughts were unspoken, they were just running through my head like a fast-forward ciné film, whilst I went in search of the letters.

"Right, "I said, "this one was written from the Grand Hotel, Stockholm. It is undated but as far as I can tell from the envelope, it looks like June 6th, 1955. The handwriting is interestingly different, kind of out of control."

Dear Marge

I have to be honest. I have tried to write many times. But it is so difficult. I cannot straighten my feelings out. It is all confusion.

Not that I do not cherish the memory of our week in London. That was beyond words – and I will not flatten its memory by formulating a description.

I have also been happy to get your two beautiful letters – the strongest ones I can remember. You are beautiful in them.

But after my stay in Oslo, I am afraid THAT is

not over…

I cannot change myself and I have to be myself – just as you have to be yourself. That is the paradox of our situation.

Time alone will show…

But I am with you all the time – and please accept my strength in your constant struggle.

We have to be true to ourselves.

I'll try to write more later – and explain.

In the meantime, all my love

Din, Odd

P.S. The seagulls over the North Sea brought back our "Ebb Tide". It constantly comes back to me – and fills me with beautiful emotions.

(Enclosed was another short note you had written earlier)

Flying Scotsman

A few words from Scotland before we embark. We have just passed the Scottish border and everything is kissed by the sun. The pastures are green and lush and my party is in high spirits.

I have had such a busy time since I left you that little thinking has been 'exercised'. I only feel at the bottom of my heart that the time we had together was very giving – and that I am missing you…

I hope that you are alright.

"After that last letter of yours, I'm afraid I rather fell apart. When you had been with me in London, somehow I couldn't quite grasp that it was the end because we were still being so loving to each other – but after reading "…I am afraid THAT is not over", finally I accepted that a parting of the ways was inevitable. And even if you didn't yet know 'where it was going', I was not prepared to wait until you found out. I had had enough of waiting."

Odd looked pensive. "Mmmmmm…" was all he could manage. "You went off to Paris again then, didn't you?"

"Yes, I wanted to be on my own. I had developed insomnia. I went to the doctor and he prescribed sleeping pills – but they didn't work. He upped the strength until I did sleep but then I was zombie-like all the next day. So then he gave me pep pills. My system felt as if it was in an out-of-control lift. He then stopped the pep pills, reduced the strength of the sleeping pills – and suggested that a change of scene might help. I was already thinking of returning to Paris; his advice propelled me into action. I didn't have much money left but I had managed to survive in Paris before and felt sure I could do so again.

I decided to keep a journal recording my every thought in the hope that giving expression to my confusion would help me understand what had happened."

"And you sent me that journal, didn't you?"

"No, Odd, I didn't – your memory of events is not correct. In fact, you came to see me in Paris because you were worried about me. I know that is what happened because I still have that book of poems you bought me – "Toi et moi" and inside you wrote the words, "With wishes from the depth of my heart – Paris, June

1955". I told you about the journal and you asked if you could read it. When you finished reading, you said you would like to keep it. I didn't really want to part with it but it was, after all, addressed to you and so I handed it over. What happened to it?"

"I had it for a long time – it was *very* powerful. No wonder I had such a guilty conscience about you."

"*Good*," I grinned. "There was one final letter later in the summer, when you were due to be in London again with another tour, and you wrote to ask if you could see me. I don't remember anything about that meeting – blocked it I guess – but I do recall asking you to ring me – with Sigrid – when you got back to Oslo – and you did. I remember vividly speaking to you both – and wishing you every happiness. Then I put the phone down – and I think I cried for a week. Well, that's all water under the bridge."

Odd seemed to be deep in thought. "Do you think, all those years ago, we were simply in love with love?"

"An interesting question, Odd. I suppose there was an element of that. We were certainly a pair of dreamers and romantics – but then would it have been so enduring if it were just that? Tell me honestly, did you mean all those things you said in your letters?"

"Of course, I did, Marge. I wouldn't have said them otherwise. Of course I meant them – every single word."

"Well, then…

You know, it is such a shame that letter-writing has gone out of fashion – replaced, sadly, by e-mails and texting in that ridiculous apology for language."

"I do agree with you, Marge, the written word is so intimate, so special, bringing hearts together in a way the digital world could not even begin to emulate."

"When I look back I think so much of our relationship happened through letters. I do wish you had kept mine."

"So do I – now."

"There was so much separation. We have probably spent more time together this time round than when we knew each other in the 50s. Of course, when we were able to meet it was so intense, wasn't it. But we lived in a bubble."

"That's true," Odd nodded.

"And bubbles when touched from the outside have a habit of bursting," I said.

That night I was finding it difficult to sleep. Raking over those memories today had been painful. I slipped out of bed, went downstairs, poured myself a brandy and sank into an armchair. I needed to recall exactly how I had felt when Odd dropped that bombshell all those years ago. I had given him only a sanitised version.

When he told me about Sigrid, it could not have hurt more if he had plunged a knife into my heart. In fact, it felt as if my heart had actually stopped beating.

So many conflicting emotions surged through me. One part of me wanted to explode, screaming and swearing 'You bastard, how dare you mess with my emotions. After all we have meant to each other, how can you just cast our love aside?'

But I did not externalise these initial reactions. I knew better – much better.

I had my own philosophy of love. I firmly believed that in an ideal relationship, the degree of love each person feels for the other should be of the same quality and depth. If ever one partner were to have a change of heart, then far better for the other to just walk away with dignity intact. Wound-licking is better done in private.

I remembered that, after that plethora of emotions had engulfed me, finally I regained my equilibrium and was able to speak. But the only words I could muster were –

"Well, that's it then."

Odd, I recalled, looked nearly as distressed as I felt, his head in his hands, his eyes moist with tears. He told me he felt very confused. 'You and me too' I had retorted, fighting to keep the tears at bay. All that faith I had in *us,* which he had told me over and over again he shared, all his declarations of love. It was such a betrayal of everything I had believed in. Unpredictability writ large!

We had always talked about how well we understood each other. Suddenly, on that day so long, long ago, I felt incapable of understanding anything. Yet, strangely, apart from my unspoken initial reactions, I did not feel angry with Odd. It was a different emotion, deeper, more profound, an overwhelming sadness for the loss of something so beautiful.

My mind then wandered back to the day I returned to Paris. I booked in again to the little hotel I knew at the foot of Montmartre.

The new sleeping pills I had been prescribed knocked me out almost straightaway, but about three hours later I woke up feeling ghastly – and then stayed awake for the rest of the night.

The following day I spent writing in my journal. I knew I should be going to the Left Bank to sort out accommodation and renew contacts at the Alliance Française but I just could not get myself into gear. Everything seemed pointless and I was so very tired, I had not had a proper night's sleep in weeks.

That night I decided to try sleeping without any pills at all. It was hopeless. I tossed and turned, got up, went back to bed, tossed and turned, again and again. The situation was not helped by the fact that my hotel shared a light-well with the hotel next door, which was used by the ladies of the night, a group of rather mature prostitutes who were always roaming around in the street below. The raised voices, screams and moans of delight – or perhaps pain – pierced the night air and were very unsettling. I yearned for oblivion.

The more I reviewed my life as it had turned out, the more I realised I had no direction any more. I was jobless, very nearly penniless and, worst of all, I had lost my man. I felt as if I had hit rock bottom. God, I was sorry for myself! If only I could sleep, if only I could sleep, I was desperate for sleep.

Then a solution flashed through my addled brain –

I am going to take the whole bottle of pills.

Now, where did I put them?

I searched and searched, unpacked my case completely, emptied my handbag, opened drawers, looked in pockets. They were nowhere to be found.

By now it was daylight. I decided to dress and go in search of some coffee. I straightened my bed and when I moved the pillows, there were the sleeping pills! I began to laugh – and laugh – and laugh.

'For God's sake girl', that sensible inner voice of mine was saying, 'you are wallowing in your misery. Stop feeling so damned sorry for yourself. There are countless millions worse off than you. I trust that's the nearest you'll get to suicide! You stupid, stupid bitch. Get a grip! I think your Guardian Angel hid those pills. In any event, no way are you the suicidal type. Enough of the histrionics, banish the Drama Queen. There is no point clinging on to something that no longer exists. Time to put it down to experience – and move on.'

My sensible inner voice was *very* cross with me – and I did listen.

Later that day I got my accommodation arranged – back at the same students' hotel as before. It was just as awful but it was cheap. Odd had asked me to let him know my address as soon as I got settled so I sent him a postcard.

A week or so later I received a phone call from Odd, he was in Paris and we agreed to meet for a coffee. It was not an easy meeting. I didn't know whether to throw my arms around his neck, or slap his face. Of course I did neither.

"Are you all right?" he asked.

"Absolutely fine, never better" I lied.

He looked at me with such intensity, I thought I would melt. I told him I had finished writing the journal. He asked if he could read it. "If you wish" I replied "it's back at my hotel." We wandered around for a while and, when browsing in a bookshop, he bought me the book of Paul Géraldy poems.

When we got to my hotel I left him to read the journal while I went to get us something to drink. When he finished reading he asked if he could keep it.

No prizes for guessing what happened next. Whether it was the habit we couldn't break – or just the sight of the bed, I don't know.

Later, in the street, we said our goodbyes "I'll be with you in thoughts" he said. "You are a strong woman, Marge, I'm sure you'll be fine."

"Of course I will" I replied lightly. "I must dash now, I have to change as I have a date tonight" I lied – for the second time that day.

Back in my room raw emotion flooded out, and the tears would not stop. I did not feel at all 'strong' and I was far from 'fine'.

I would never have thought it possible to find greater love and beauty in a relationship than we had known. How could his feelings have changed? What had he found in Sigrid that he hadn't found in me? I will never believe anything a man says to me again. Never, never, NEVER – and my tears continued through the night.

The following morning the sun was streaming in my window. I was aware that my life had changed – there was an enormous hole in it. 'But' said that wise inner voice 'it is not the end of the world. You have your youth, your health and you are in the most beautiful city in the world. Now go out there and enjoy it!' And I did!

All these memories were so vivid, as if they happened yesterday – and the detail I can remember is quite extraordinary. However, I decided I would not share all this with Odd – in particular I would not want him to know that I came close to committing suicide. Then I pondered – if my Guardian Angel had *not* hidden those pills – would I have taken the lot? An unanswerable question. 'Rubbish' screamed my inner voice – 'resilience is your middle name!'

Okay, okay – it's time I crept back into bed – it was 3:00 a.m.

The morning came, all too soon, and it was time to pack and

leave for the airport. "When will I see you again? How about another visit to me in Trondheim?"

"I'd love to – October perhaps? I have a very busy September but, having said that, if you need me, just phone and I'll be on the next flight, whatever."

"My lovely girl," he said.

Chapter 15

He called me as soon as he got home just to report that he was safely back and the journey had been without incident. I told him he had left all sorts of things behind – books, money, toiletries, socks, shirt. "No matter," he said. "I'll be back again in the early spring. It is said, isn't it, that if people leave things behind, it is because they want to return?"

"Yes, something like that," I replied.

Odd told me he was going to spend the next week, or however long it took, working on the films he had taken in order to produce a DVD for me. He was hoping that an audio-visual friend of his would lend a hand.

Each day, we spoke on the phone – and usually more than once. He seemed to be in fairly good spirits and was optimistic that the next course of chemotherapy would help his condition. He gave me the dates of when it would be – but then just after starting it he had another fall at home in the flat. It sounded as if it had cancelled out all the progress he had made under Simon's care. He also confessed that he was finding eating ever more difficult.

A few days later, there was a message from him on my answering service, saying, "I am so weak, Marge. I am so very weak. I can hardly stand up." When I rang him back the first thing he said was that he was so sorry he had left me such a miserable message.

"I should not have worried you like that, it was just a particularly bad night, no sleep at all, and then an even worse morning. This evening, however, I am not too bad. The visiting nurse came – they have modified my medication and I am back on morphine for the pain – so don't worry, my lovely girl."

I was not convinced. "Odd, how about a visit from your Marge, next week?"

"I must confess that sounds good. I will ask my friend, Arne, to do the driving and we will meet you at the airport."

It was clear from the following days' phone calls that there had been some deterioration. The night before I was due to leave, I had a call from Odd around midnight saying he didn't feel he could make the journey to the airport but that Arne would be there to meet me.

Everything went according to plan until we got to Odd's flat. Worryingly, there were no lights visible and no response to our knocking on the door. We contacted the immediate neighbours who had a key and I was ushered into their flat for a coffee while the men went into Odd's flat to see what had happened. There he was naked on the floor but still conscious and able to tell them what had transpired.

Very soon after he rang me, he had had a shower (which meant he had taken off the emergency alarm he had been given), got into bed and then promptly fell out of bed with a bang. He was too weak and in too much pain to get himself up and so there he had stayed all night and all the following day: it was now 5.30 p.m. Mercifully, the flat was well heated but it was all an awful shock (for *everyone*, need I add). They rang straight away for an ambulance and got some clothes on him. The first I saw of him was on a stretcher being carried into the ambulance. He was calling out, "Where's Marge? I want my Marge."

"I'm here, Odd, and coming with you in the ambulance." I gave him a big hug and told him there had been no need to stage such a drama just to make my arrival memorable! He enjoyed the joke and it was good to see he was still capable of laughing.

The hospital plus the care and attention he was given were impressive. Odd was thoroughly x-rayed, blood samples were taken and he was seen and examined by four different doctors during the course of the night. He was put to bed in a well-equipped and comfortable room with en-suite bathroom. He asked the nurse if I could stay the night with him and she seemed to think it would be alright. However, the consultant said it was out of the question. It must have been nearly 1:00 a.m. by the time I left Odd. My first task was to find my way out of the hospital – all the doors were locked – and I couldn't find anyone to ask. Then I heard some footsteps – someone else had been visiting late. She spoke English *and* she knew the code for opening the door but wasn't sure where I would find a taxi. I hadn't a clue where I was, it was snowing hard and it was icy and slippery underfoot. I walked around the hospital grounds for ages until finally I found a sign saying 'Taxis'. There weren't any but I waited and waited and eventually one turned up.

By the time I got to Odd's flat, I was frozen and exhausted, physically and emotionally, as well as being somewhat light-headed having not eaten all day. But when I walked in the door, my spirits lifted. In the hall, there was a large vase of the most utterly beautiful roses to welcome me – and in the kitchen one perfect red rose.

I glanced at the photos on the wall – Sigrid of course, one of Marie in her 20s and now Marge as well. The many shades of love I mused.

The fridge and cupboards were bursting with food and booze and there was a large bowl of fruit on the table. In the living room, I noticed there were a couple of framed photographs of the two of us from his Kentish visit – and yes, my friends were right – we really did look like a couple! On top of that, he had acquired a bed for me which was cosily made up awaiting my arrival and he had even bought me a set of smart new towels. Bless him, in spite of all his health issues, he had gone to so much trouble to welcome me.

When I had stayed there previously, I slept on the sofa. The hospital had insisted that he exchange his normal bed for a hospital bed – which was alright for two for a cuddle but not for sleeping. It had worried him that I slept on the sofa (even though I insisted that it was comfortable) – hence the new acquisition.

The following morning, I gathered together the clothes, books and writing materials that he felt he might need in hospital. When I arrived, to my surprise, Odd was up, dressed and sitting in an armchair in his room – waiting for me with a broad smile on his face.

"Come close, Marge. I want you very, very close to me." We sat holding hands, talking and laughing.

"I wanted this visit of yours to be special. I am so sorry I was stupid enough to fall out of bed – I suppose it had something to do with all those pills I'm taking."

By late afternoon, I could see that he was having a delayed reaction to his ordeal of the previous day. (I had noticed also that he had lost more weight since his visit to me in August.) It was time to get him back into bed and I left him to get some rest – and returned to the flat. It was so strange to be there without Odd – not at all the way he had planned it. Well, as the saying goes, "When the play is in full flow, you can't change the script."

I knew I should cook myself a proper meal – he had bought so much food for me – but I didn't feel like cooking or eating for that matter. Instead, I opened a bottle of red wine – and a packet of cigarettes (the flat was still heavy with a smoker's habit). I put on one of our favourite CDs and went off into some kind of reverie. I tried to imagine Odd's life in this flat with Sigrid. "Everybody loved her" he had told me. There were many photographs – and a couple of fine paintings of Sigrid. I am sure she was a beautiful woman – in all ways. With hindsight – and maturity – I guess I must concede that in all probability, he made the right choice.

I then pondered what it might have been like if we had got together. Although he was a dreamer, he also had his practical side. When he wasn't writing me love letters romanticising about our future together, he *must* have had some concerns about how a foreigner like me would take to the Norwegian way of life. He would have been mindful of the fact that I had been brought up in a hot, sunny country, so how would I have coped with all that snow and ice? Winters are long in Norway with much shorter hours of daylight, which could be depressing.

Then, of course, Norwegians are such sporty, outdoor types. Would I have been able to keep up? I never thought of myself as overly sporty (perhaps I was rather better at indoor sports!) I had loved my brief experience of the mountains but I was only a beginner at skiing. How long would it have taken me to become really proficient?

Then there was the question of language. Everyday life would not have been too much of a problem, as most of them speak English, but in terms of getting an interesting job, I am sure I would have needed to speak fluent Norwegian – and that would have taken years. Right occupation is so important. I had always felt there was a meaningful role for me to play if only I could find it. The career that I did carve out for myself in the UK would not have been possible for me in Norway. Running a school was hard work, long hours and challenging, but I loved every minute of it.

At the time, of course, I didn't give a moment's consideration to any of these practical issues – although now I can see that similar backgrounds and shared interests should not be ignored. He was certainly at the crossroads in June 1955, and having had such an unfortunate experience of marriage already, he would not have wanted to make another mistake.

I knew I was his dream for some four years – he told me often enough – but perhaps of the two of us, I was the bigger dreamer. Anyway, whatever thought processes went on in his head, it was Sigrid who won the day – and I suppose that was exactly the way it was meant to be. What a moment of clarity!

Well, that's history. What matters now is that our paths have crossed again and we are so enjoying this 'us time' – however short or long it may be.

I poured myself another glass of wine and let my mind wander back to when we broke up. My life-long habit of always trying to turn negatives into positives was not too successful at that time. Parting from Odd engulfed me in such a deep feeling of loss that I struggled to find anything positive in the situation – unless one could count as a positive the painful realisation of the impermanence of all things. Now that was a good life-lesson to take on board. Having drowned in each other's love for so long – in words written and spoken, in deeds, in physical expression, in the 'certainty' that we belonged to each other – it was so damned difficult to accept that it had come to an end.

If I had been a damsel living in Victorian times, I might have sued him for breach of promise! What a ridiculous custom that was. You can't *make* someone love you, any more than you can reheat a soufflé. If it's over, it's over – better to let go gracefully. I suppose some women would have ranted and raved. After all, I had waited for him for four years whilst he was forced/tricked into marriage with a woman he didn't love, became the father of a child he didn't want, followed by the painful drawn-out process of getting her agreement to a divorce. Then, just as the divorce was about to become a reality, he met Sigrid.

That last long period of separation we had had to endure undoubtedly led to extreme loneliness. As in all areas of life, if there is a vacuum, it gets filled.

There was no point in fighting it. I didn't have an iceberg's chance in hell of changing anything. I knew he had not gone looking for someone else, it just happened. 'Life is what happens when you are planning other things' came to mind again.

I was not jealous of Sigrid – jealousy is such a destructive emotion, nor was I angry with Odd – it wasn't like that. There were no harsh words exchanged, indeed right up until our final farewell, we were still being so loving to each other. It felt more like the ending of a chapter in our lives, but it left me feeling empty, as if I had lost part of myself, and life was suddenly monochromatic and pointless. It would have been impossible for me to be angry with Odd; for me he was synonymous with beauty, we had experienced such heights together – but, let's face it, love does not come with a guarantee!

To accompany my third (or was it the fourth?) glass of wine, I started wondering what might have happened if the situation had been reversed. For example, during that long period of being apart when circumstances dictated a reduced flow of letters as well, supposing a mutual friend had introduced me to Robert. What would have happened? It's impossible to answer – but perhaps *I* would have been the one to walk away. Who knows? And how would Odd have reacted? Another question came into my mind: what would have happened if we had met again when both our spouses were still alive? Now that's one to be pondered!

The 'what if' game is a road to nowhere, but it's interesting nonetheless.

In spite of all my philosophising at the time, telling myself I was a survivor, a glass half-full kind of a girl, with a love of life that would see me through – in actual fact, I was devastated and utterly confused.

My mind wandered back to those five years from when Odd left me until I married Tom – what I tend to think of now as my feral period!

I guess when you are young, you are ill-equipped to deal with mega disappointment. I am the first to admit that I was a late developer so, for sure, I had some growing up to do – and, yes, possibly a few wild oats to sow as well. Even if I had a somewhat flirtatious personality, essentially I was a one-man woman – but anyone who knew me during the late 1950s would never have believed that! Of course, I knew I had to accept the hand I had been dealt, nevertheless, I felt mightily rebellious.

I decided to concentrate on building myself a career. I had been in life's waiting room long enough. Having done the appropriate courses in journalism and public relations, I decided it was the path for me.

Of course, that particular milieu almost issued an invitation to live life in the fast lane, which was well suited to my frame of mind at the time. I was only 26, a free spirit and, now, responsible only to myself. Sure, I would make some mistakes – so what! I reasoned that this was the time in my life when I could – and would – risk-take. However, this crazy mindset into which I had drifted led me into a never-ending string of relationships. I was like a feather in the wind, blowing hither and thither.

I had umpteen proposals of marriage. In retrospect, I think there was an unconscious mechanism at work, a strong desire to get my own back on men in general. The result was that I turned into something of a heartbreaker. With each new relationship, I would fool myself that at long last I had found Mr Right. Then, after becoming engaged, I would come to my senses – and call it off! The trouble was that Odd was the one man against whom I measured all other men and – for me – they were all found wanting. All that clinging to the past had trapped me in a nightmare entirely of my own making. I had become an emotional cripple, incapable of any kind of long-term commitment to anyone. I can still blush when I recall my stupidity.

On the work front, however, I was doing well. I had a good, well-paid job. I also had a newly-decorated flat which I loved, a wide circle of friends and a hectic social life, all of which should have made me happy; but life felt hollow and unsatisfying. I was lost, I needed grounding and I yearned for some kind of spiritual path. Eventually I found my way to Buddhism – and that is when I began to get my life back on track.

Everything happens for a reason, even if the reason is not clear at the time. Supposing I had married Odd, my life would have been completely different – well, obviously. However, thinking in broader terms, if, as a result, I had not met and married Tom, then the school which we co-founded would never have come into being. What ramifications that would have had! Then, too, if my marriage to Tom had not fallen apart then I would not have got together with my Robert … One could continue this line of thought ad infinitum. My reflections were now darting off in all directions – due no doubt to having finished the whole bottle of wine all on my own – and on an empty stomach.

It was time for bed and, as I drifted off, I told myself how grateful I was for my life, no regrets at all. It has been so full of wonderful happenings and wonderful people – and it still is! I recalled that in a letter some five months ago about our meeting again, Odd had written, "I have a feeling that we feel very much the same way. This was life's reward to both of us." Indeed it was.

On that happy note, I turned over and – to my surprise – fell out of bed! What is it about this flat?!

Chapter 16

In the morning, the sun was doing its best to put in an appearance. The ground was still icy but there hadn't been any more snow. When I got to the hospital, Odd told me right away that the results of the blood test left much to be desired. They were keeping him in hospital but told him his general state was such that they could not restart the chemotherapy at present. I asked him to promise that he would not hold anything back from me – and he agreed, adding that he would tell me everything the moment he was given information, whether good or bad.

To lighten the mood, I told Odd that I had made a start on 'our story' and I read him the first ten pages. He liked the way I had set the scene and felt that my style of writing was exactly right for a special love story. When we had discussed the idea of writing the book, back in August, we agreed that the best place to start was when we met again. Then, through the letters, the past could be revealed gradually and the present, of course, would be recorded when it happened. The ending would no doubt write itself. It is said, I recalled, that a happy ending is only *where* you decide to stop your story.

Odd pointed out that everyone – on both sides of the North Sea – to whom we had told our story, really loved it. He was convinced therefore that the book could help people. "Furthermore," he said, "a true story such as ours is so life-affirming – and, Marge, you must tell it openly and honestly, exactly the way it happened – no need to embellish, no need to conceal – and, of course, you have my permission to quote all my letters. It is important for the reader to feel the emotional pulse."

That afternoon, Roger, a friend of Odd's, called in and he too listened to my reading of the beginning of our book. He said he wanted to order a copy right away. The three of us then discussed possible titles and I read out the list I had cobbled together that morning: Echoes of the Past, The Reawakening, Full Circle, The Letters, First Love, Last Love, Lost and Found, Past and Present, Rediscovering Love, Pieces of Life, Revisiting Love, Connected. After much talk, 'Full Circle' won the vote.

Each day of my stay I spent with Odd at the hospital. He had lots of visitors and it was obvious that he was much loved by his friends.

Some of the time, we worked on translating his Cyprus poems. When he felt tired, he would rest while I continued with the book. It was great to be doing something literary together once again. It reminded me of the James Bridie thesis days, when I was able to research material for Odd in London which wasn't readily available in Norway. But, the Scottish playwright to one side, we both loved

198

the theatre so much. Often I would see a play in London which was also on in Oslo. We were then able to discuss it and compare our reactions.

Watching him sleeping, I remembered how much he had encouraged me with my studies in those far-off days. He really understood how 'cheated' I felt that I had not gone on to university as planned, due to my Father's illness and death which presented many problems for the family. It was not just the grief and loss, but all sorts of financial complications as well concerning the business. Fortunately, my Mother was introduced to a high-flying financial consultant who, in the end, got everything sorted out – but it took a couple of years, and during that time, we had no idea what the outcome would be – so university was no longer an option. Instead, I took a business course and then got a job. My long-held desire to travel also had to retire to the back burner.

All these memories were running through my mind as I looked at my Odd sleeping peacefully. He was, I reflected, a born teacher – and poet. There must be so many grateful former students of his in Trondheim. On my previous visit, every time we went out we seemed to bump into someone he had taught. And what makes a good teacher? I pondered. I had attended one of his English language classes in Oslo many moons ago, and remembered thinking to myself what a compelling presence he had, an authority that totally held his students' attention. When you couple those qualities with a wonderful speaking-voice and his capacity to connect with people, then you have a *very* good teacher. Since retiring from his academic career, he had returned to his life-long passion for poetry, for Odd a form of life. Although he had always written poems, it is interesting that he never thought about publishing them until he was in his seventies – and then they were very well received. However, it's his last book of poems, "Betenkningstid", about facing death and reviewing his life, that received rave reviews in the Press. How wonderful, I thought, to be highly acclaimed for doing something you love doing.

He was stirring now and when he opened his eyes, the first thing he said to me was, "Marge, I can't begin to tell you how much sunshine you have brought to me. I'm such a lucky boy."

"What a lovely thing to say, Odd, but I'm afraid you will be losing your sunshine tomorrow, which is when I have my flight home."

"Well, let's make the most of the time we have left. I am going to get up now and sit in the armchair and I want you to sit very close to me, and tell me some more about your eventful life. I don't know much of what it was like for you growing up in Australia."

"Well, for sure I had an easier time than you did in German-occupied Narvik."

"Yes, they were difficult years. I seem to remember you telling me that you felt you didn't belong in Australia."

"That's right. I always felt like an alien in the country of my birth. Strange, huh? Perhaps it had something to do with my preference as a young kid for reading the National Geographic magazine rather than comics. From the youngest age, I dreamt of travelling. In my last year at school, we were all wide-eyed and bushy-tailed about what the future would hold for each of us, and one girl suggested meeting up in ten years' time on the steps of the Post Office in Melbourne and bringing our husbands and children with us. 'Not this girl,' I shouted. 'I'll be somewhere else in the world – and definitely not married with children. There's so much I want to see, experience and learn.' I guess my unquenchable thirst for life was apparent even then – and it has never left me."

"And I hope it never will, Marge – and, please, never lose your spontaneity or your spirit of adventure. It's who you are."

"You know, Odd, I was aware always that I had been blessed with a sort of bottomless pit of energy and so I knew I was going to be one of life's participators, rather than taking a back seat. I felt I would find something important to do, eventually, but I had no idea what it might be."

"Well, my lovely girl, you did indeed find the right vehicle for your talents. Co-founding the European School of Osteopathy was such a big and far-reaching achievement. I loved your book. But take me back to your life in Australia."

"During the war, it was the Japanese that *we* feared. After all, they bombed Darwin in the Northern Territory – and then there was a submarine in Sydney Harbour. It was all getting too close for comfort. I recall my Father suddenly buying a cottage in the hills far away from the city of Melbourne, the plan being that, if the situation worsened, we would decamp. There was talk at the time of children being evacuated, which my Mother would have hated, hence my Dad's speedy purchase – but it never came to that. There was a crazy exercise that my school dreamt up which still makes me smile. Each pupil had to make a hole through a cork and then thread through a long piece of string. We were asked to wear this at all times around our neck under our school blouse. At various unexpected moments during the following months, the music teacher would hit a rather large gong, which was the signal for us all to rush out of our classrooms and down to the playing fields with our corks in our mouths! The idea, I seem to recall, was that if there was an air raid, the cork would stop us biting our tongue. Realistically, if a bomb was about to fall, surely biting your tongue would be the least of your worries! However, apart from that somewhat loony episode, I really loved school – and did well too, finishing up Dux of the School in my final year. I don't think the term Dux is used in Europe, is it? It just means top pupil academically in a school.

My sister, you may recall, was eight years older than me. During the war, she belonged to a Forces Club where overseas servicemen were entertained and introduced to Australian families. We used to have a group of Americans to lunch every Sunday and when they had some leave, we would take them to the sea or the country for a family picnic or perhaps a round of golf with my Dad. We made some wonderful friends and there was one in particular with whom my sister fell madly in love – and, secretly, so did I – aged 14! He was a lieutenant in the army and devastatingly handsome. I remember he gave me an American coin, a cent, and I had it mounted on a chain and used to wear it around my neck. At the end of the war, he returned home – and married his former sweetheart – much to the disappointment of my sister, and the whole family! However, we kept in touch with him and when, years later, Mother and I visited the USA, we wrote to say we would love to see him. There was an enthusiastic reply inviting us to stay with them for the weekend. As it happened, our visit coincided with Thanksgiving Day. In the morning, we were taken on a long drive to see the sights and on our return at lunchtime, there was the most wonderful surprise. Seated with his family around the *very* large dining table were four other former soldiers whom we had entertained many times during the war, together with their wives. What a heart-warming reunion it was.

Another wartime memory I have was my performing period. I had, like many children, piano and singing lessons, as well as attending classes in ballet and tap dancing. I gathered around me my most talented chums and formed a little theatre company. I used to write all the material and design the costumes for our mothers to make, and then we would put on a concert to raise money for the Red Cross. I guess I must have been quite a little show-off – but I did so enjoy it all.

"Tell me about the men in your life."

"All of them?" I said, aghast.

"Well, let's start with the main ones."

"Then I must begin with my Father. Dad was such a wonderful role model, the kindest and most caring of men and loved by everyone, especially my Mother. They were lovebirds throughout their marriage.

"Whenever someone had a problem, it was always my Dad they would turn to – whether one of the family, a friend or a member of his staff. Let me give you an example that illustrates his kindness.

"One night – gone midnight – the telephone rang; we were all in bed asleep. It was a friend of my sister who had recently become engaged and she was away on holiday with her fiancé. The poor girl was in a terrible state. They had gone swimming in the sea at dusk and had the misfortune to be pursued by a shark. She escaped but her fiancé was attacked and killed. His bloody torso was later washed up on the shore. Just imagine the horror of it all. She was an orphan, having lost both parents in a car crash when she was 15. Ever since, I think she came to regard my Dad as a surrogate father. Of course, he responded immediately to her distress and drove through the night, over 100 miles, to where she was staying. He brought her back home and she stayed with us for ages.

"Not only was my Father a man of high principle in his personal life, but in business as well. He instilled in me a sense of values, justice and the importance of truth in all one's dealings. I am so grateful he was my Dad."

"It is lovely to hear you speak with such warmth about your Father. So who was the next man of significance in your life?"

"Well, there was this Norwegian I met…"

"Oh, really, Marge … so who came after me then?"

"From when we parted until I married my first husband, Tom, I confess I played the field. I don't think we have enough time for me to relate all of my escapades during those five feral years, but I guess I could tell you about some of the main players – not necessarily in chronological order, just as the memories occur to me.

"Let me see, there was Pietro – typically Italian and mind-blowingly handsome. When I met him, it was lust at first sight for both of us. After some six months, he asked me to marry him.

"All went well for several weeks – until, by chance, I discovered he was still seeing his previous girlfriend! MEN! A wave of unaccustomed cynicism flooded over me. 'That's it – we are finished – please do not contact me again,' I said with barely-controlled anger.

"Some three months later, we bumped into each other in Chelsea. We chatted, drifted into a bar, and chatted some more. He told me he was full of remorse for what had happened and would I consider giving him a second chance, as he still loved me. The old Italian charm was operating at full throttle! I succumbed and we started seeing each other again – and, unbelievably, we became engaged for the second time.

"It wasn't sensible the first time, and it was nothing short of insane the second time (I think my inner voice must have been on holiday!).

"A girl pal of mine, who used to refer to him as the Italian Stallion, said to me, 'For God's sake call it off. He may be stupendous in the bedroom, but as a full-time partner, he would be hell.' She was right of course, and eventually I did end it – but we remained good friends. In fact, when I married Tom, he came to the wedding.

"Of course, you know about my 'other Norwegian', don't you? That story was a little bit like us, but in reverse and with less drama. I think I was his first real woman and, for sure, I was his first big love. He adored me, I knew that – and I left him in the midst of the wedding preparations in Oslo. What a cruel thing to do. Although I didn't act as I did on a conscious level, I do wonder whether somewhere deep down inside I was trying to get my own back on all things Norwegian. How appalling! What is that saying? 'What goes round, comes round.' Anyway, that is yet another episode from my wild years of which I am thoroughly ashamed.

"Thank goodness I never got involved in drug-taking. There wasn't nearly so much of it in the 50s. Although, come to think of it, I did have a brief encounter with a chemical substance. At a PR-Advertising Agency I was working at, the whole team used to take a tablet that was available over the counter from the chemist. It was intended for slimmers as it suppressed the appetite; however, it also gave you a high. If there was a meeting with a client, we would all have one of the tablets and then, my goodness, the creative juices would flow! Clients never failed to be impressed with our dynamism. The trouble was the after-effects of those awful pills – extreme thirst, headache and muzziness. At the time, I was going out with one of the Account Executives and, after one such client meeting, we went out to dinner, not realising at the time that alcohol after one of those pills was NOT a good idea. After only a bottle of wine between the two of us, we were legless. There was no way he could drive his car, it was teeming with rain and not a taxi in sight, so we decided to go back to the office. As we often worked late we both had keys. There was a flat on the top floor reserved for the use of one of our overseas clients. We managed to get upstairs and then passed out on the bed. About three in the morning, the overseas client arrived – unannounced – with a lady friend. Embarrassment all round. The following morning our boss gave us – a deserved – telling-off and I thought we might get the sack. But in the end he gave us a broad smile and said, 'To be honest, I would have done the same thing in the circumstances.'"

"What else do you want to know, Odd?"

"I want to hear everything about your life. Tell me a bit more about your Mother, I remember her well. A pretty woman with quite a bubbly personality; but I recall you saying that she was rather possessive, is that right?"

"When I was young, she was very protective of me but, after my father died, she gradually became more possessive – so that it felt more like 'Smother Love'. I think the protective bit was heightened by a very nasty experience I had when I was 12. I was playing in the park, near our home, with some girlfriends when we were chased by a group of 16-17 year old boys. I got caught and dragged into the bushes – with the object of a 'gang bang' in their nasty little minds. I was terrified – but just as the worst was about to happen, I was rescued by a man who was walking through the park. My girlfriends had alerted him to my plight and he came running and scared them off – not a moment too soon! Of course, my Mother was upset by the thought of what nearly happened to her daughter – hence the over-protectiveness.

Years later, after my Father's death, she was well aware of my long-held desire to travel and that was when she decided to take me on a year-long round-the-world trip for my 21st birthday – some present, eh? Dad had left her well provided for and, of course, she also wanted to travel. I must say we did have an incredible year. However, bless her heart, she had a long-term plan. She was sure that the trip would rid me of my travel bug and I would then be content to marry some nice Australian man, live somewhere near her and have lots of children. The trouble was *my* plans could not have been more different. I was more convinced than ever that my future would be in Europe, not Australia, and I was desperate to be free and independent. On top of all that, I had met you, Odd, and so I had more than one reason to return to Europe. As they say, the rest is history."

Chapter 17

As soon as I got home, I rang Odd to see how he was and the answer was: "I miss you, I miss you, I miss you."

"And, I miss you too," I said. "How are things?"

"Not too good, Marge. I'm due to see the consultant. I wanted to work on the poems but I couldn't find the energy today."

For the next three months, November to January, we spoke on the phone every single day – and sometimes in the middle of the night as well. We covered every imaginable subject – and emotion.

Before leaving Trondheim, Odd had given me the DVD of his visit to Kent. It was – and still is – so wonderful to relive those happy weeks we had together.

I knew he must be suffering not only physically, but from the blackest boredom as well, having spent so long in hospital. In order to help him feel that life was still happening during this period of 'incarceration', I decided to try by every means to promote his poetry by making it accessible to a much wider audience. I felt this would provide some stimulation. It is so important to feel you are living, even if you know you are dying. I had discussed his Cyprus poems with my dear Greek-Cypriot friends whom Odd had met when he was staying with me. Martino Tirimo took action. He contacted the editor of "In Focus" magazine, which is sponsored by the Cyprus PEN Centre and distributed worldwide to universities, libraries, etc. Martino explained how Odd had spent every winter in Cyprus over a 10 year period, during which he had developed a great affection for the island, and this was reflected in his books of poems, some of which were now being translated into English. He also told the editor that Odd had been diagnosed with inoperable stomach cancer in 2009 and, rather than just waiting to die, he gathered his courage and wrote a further and highly-acclaimed book of poetry about facing death and reviewing his life.

Martino also contacted "Cyprus Today", another cultural magazine. In an e-mail, he wrote: "I feel extremely fortunate to have met such a wonderful human being and have happy memories of the stimulating discussions we had together, a most cultured man who loved Cyprus very deeply."

It was then over to me to provide the biographical notes, photographs and, of course, the poems. Each additional Cyprus poem that Odd translated was typed by his friend, Arne-Jørgen, who then sent it to me for discussion with Odd by telephone. Sometimes I could suggest a slightly better word or phrase. We did so enjoy collaborating in this way, just as we had done during his stay with me.

When I rang him and asked for a biographical piece for the magazine, it was on one of his not-so-good days and so he asked me to have a go at writing it. I rang back that evening to read it to him, at the end of which there was a stunned silence. "Marge, I did manage to put pen to paper late this afternoon and the extraordinary thing is that we have both written virtually the same text – there is hardly any difference. Amazing!"

The response from both magazines was enthusiastic. The Editor of "In Focus" wrote: "…I have read his biographical note and was deeply moved. This man is a Hero, a brilliant example for people who face serious health problems with the threat of death. I have also read his poems and was moved even more deeply, establishing how much this beautiful man of the distant cold north has loved our little country, its nature, its beauties, its history."

It was a joy to be able to keep Odd informed of all these activities. He was so thrilled with each new development. For example, we were warmly invited to visit Cyprus, as soon as he was well enough to travel, as they wanted him to give a poetry reading at a reception they would arrange to honour him. There was also talk about finding a suitable person to translate his poems into Greek and publishing them in a booklet. In addition, his friend, Marie, was translating them into French. In the UK, I got in touch with the Anglo-Norse Society (of which I was once a member) with the suggestion of a poetry reading by Odd on his next visit to the UK. Odysseus and Anna suggested an evening event at the Hellenic Centre in London with Martino playing the piano and Odd reading his poems.

I also rang the Poetry Society and the journal "Poetry Today" and Martino made contact with the organisers of the Poetry Festival. It was all happening – and Odd told me he felt it was helping him in his battle. He said he now had so much to look forward to and added, "You will come everywhere with me, Marge, won't you?"

"Try and stop me!" I replied.

There was already another possibility of travel for us. The hospital had a branch, for want of a better word, in Spain – a sort of Rest Home. Odd liked the idea of some winter sunshine and he asked if I would meet him there. He felt it would be far better for me, rather than coming back to Trondheim in mid-winter.

He was worried about me being all on my own in his flat and having to cope with travelling to and from the hospital, shopping for food etc, in severe snow and ice, and so we agreed that I would join him in Alicante. From enquiries he made, it appeared that I could stay with him in the Rest Home, which would be ideal. He booked a three-week stay and his flight. Deep down I wondered whether any of our plans would reach fruition – and I'm sure that thought also crossed his mind – but we remained optimistic and ever-hopeful of the power of positive thought. It was always a bonus if I could say something that would make him laugh but I must confess that trying to be humorous when one's heart is heavy is quite challenging – I guess he felt the same way.

Thinking about it, in those far off days, we got to really know each other through our letters, whereas the process of rediscovering each other this time round owed much to the telephone. However, one day, Odd said he felt like writing to me – and he did.

Trondheim, November 17th 2010
My dear Marge!

To sit with my pen, between you and me.

211

My pen which is so full of words existing for you, only for you. My pen, my instrument of contact with your soul and your heart.

All these weeks, all this time, my instrument has not been tuned to the music which is within me, and which exists for you only and there is a sadness when I cannot feel that we tremble together like we did when we were together in the music.

I feel that this is a bit 'soft' but I have to put it this way because there is so much that has not been said during all this time we were not together.

When will I be able to say all that ought to be said to you, all you deserve to hear. That is how I feel it now. But I know that you and me are so alike in the sense that we love each other, because we feel so much, especially when we act similarly – and that is what we do so often.

Take the biographical thing for Martino. You wrote very nearly the same words as me. It is amazing, Margino, must I not love a person who is so like myself? I think you even put the commas in the same place, perhaps determined by Buddha or some other god.

You probably discover that my daily dose of medicine is a bit over the 'edge' for my brain, and my head works in an unusual way. Each line takes ever more energy, and my sorrow is genuine when I discover everything I am unable to write down.

So much happens here too which ought to be recorded – like this one. Last night a man entered my room in darkness and got into bed with me. I chased him out and away he went – stealing my socks and shirt. Then at breakfast, some old ladies wanted to shut out the sun and I shouted, Up with the blind at once! We are going to be in the darkness so terribly long. Give me the *light*! (Goethe). And all the dumb ones – they sit down in front of you, and gradually disappear within themselves. Amazing.

Today I saw the doctor. My state of health is not good enough to continue my treatment but we discussed some 'improvements' like better nourishment, more exercise etc, so let us hope.

Marge, nobody must be allowed to take this away from us. You my lovely girl.

Yours, Odd

PS Tonight, when I go to bed, I will ask my imagination to create the most tender dreams of love and affection about you and me. You, finally in my arms. Thus, we will disappear in veils of lovely feelings. Your Odd

Boxley, November 22nd 2010

My dear special man

We have just spoken on the telephone – and I sit here on my (our!) bed marvelling at technology! All I do is press a few buttons and instantly I hear your voice from the other side of the North Sea by means of an even smaller piece of equipment that fits into the palm of your hand. So clever, isn't it!

Then I think back to that momentous day in Narvik when – on a whim – I wandered into the Tourist Office and, Hey Presto, the Internet produced your telephone number in minutes. How extraordinary was that! I must MUST drag myself into the 21st century very soon by making friends with the laptop computer which sits unused and unloved on my desk.

No matter how impressive technology is, you can't beat a handwritten letter for conveying feelings – and I loved your recent letter which reduced me to tears.

Speaking of writing, I continue, somewhat sporadically, with our story. I do hope, when you are feeling better, you will be able to contribute to the manuscript. It will add enormously to the book. I know you agree to the inclusion of your letters, but it would be great to have your 2010 thoughts and feelings as well.

Thinking about our 'journey' it seems to me to have all the elements of a cracking good story: surprise, joy, discovery, sadness, love, poignancy, sex, humour, tenderness. Then of course there is our much-prized openness, the freedom to express exactly what we think and feel, plus the joy of rediscovering the similarities between us on so many levels. AMAZING! As everyone says, it would make a great film – and, who knows, it might even happen. Life is full of surprises. You just have to be open to all possibilities and believe in the power of positive thought.

Well, enough of my ramblings for now.

You said you wanted a letter at both addresses, so I'll

continue in no.2

Always

Your Marge

Kjare, dear Marge

To open a letter, without a letter inside is a disappointment -- therefore this little note to tell you that I send two DVDs separately because there is not enough room in the one envelope.

Secondly, to visualise that I have placed my heart.

I await a visit from Arne Jørgen, my wonderful friend, who will mail my post to you.

Your, Odd

Boxley, Letter no. 2, November 23rd 2010

Dear One

Here I am again. I wonder which letter will reach you first.

From our conversation this morning I was so pleased to hear they have confirmed that it will be alright for you to go to Spain, if you are well enough to make the journey. What a wonderful thought, three weeks together in the sun.

Thank you for encouraging me to try my hand at writing poetry. I now enclose my first effort – please feel free to criticise it as much as you like! How lucky I am to have the guidance of someone who has truly mastered such a wonderful art form.

Joy oh joy, the mail has just arrived with the other DVD,

plus such a sweet letter from my Odd, whose heart I have kissed! I love the box cover you have done for the DVD – both the title 'Paradise Regained' and the photograph of the two of us, not forgetting the little bunch of red roses on the label.

All for now.

Big hugs

Your Marge

As the weeks rolled by, we continued to discuss, by telephone and letters, so many different topics, as well as exploring our own inner landscapes. We also talked about our sixth sense, that whole universe that is inside us – perhaps the one we got lost in when we listened to beautiful music together with the whole of our being. Trembling in the music, as Odd put it.

During one of our middle-of-the-night telephone conversations, Odd said, "Tell me some more about your wild times in London."

"Well, I think the swinging 60s started, for me, in 1955, after we were no longer together. I guess I was always a bit ahead of my time!

"One of my friends, a talented artist, moved in exalted circles and she introduced me to her social scene: a heady mix of artists, actors, playwrights, models and titled people, including a Marquis or two who were always appearing in the social pages of the press. I went out for a while with the son of an Earl. I attended some amazing parties, balls and musical soirées. It was such an exciting time to be in London and be a part of the creative social set. It was the era of the 'Angry Young Men' heralded by John Osborne's acclaimed play, 'Look Back in Anger'.

"There were quite a few weirdos around then too and there were those who seemed to delight in 'shocking' whether in dress, behaviour or sexual exploits."

"Give me an example, Marge."

"Let me think. Oh, yes, there was a guy to whom I was introduced who gave the impression of being the perfect English gentleman – Eton and Oxford educated, immaculate in dress and manner. He looked like the Hollywood star, Cary Grant, and he was every bit as suave.

"He invited me to dinner at the Savoy. The evening was most enjoyable until we got back to my flat when he seemed to metamorphose into someone I did not like one little bit. He said he wanted to introduce me to the sexual excitement of sado-masochism. I was dumbfounded. Before I could get my breath back, he had removed his leather belt and was whipping me with it! What a disappointment he turned out to be. As SM held no appeal for me, I soon got rid of him."

"Now, tell me, Marge, about a *nice* experience you had during this period."

"There were many, of course, but one springs to mind which I am sure you will like. A journalist friend, who had connections with the New York Times, introduced me to a theatre critic who was over from the States in order to see the best that London had to offer in the theatre.

"We hit it off straight away and as a result he invited me to join him over the next ten days of theatre-going. I was in heaven – a different play every evening followed by a stimulating discussion of the performance over supper in various top restaurants. What a lucky girl I was. There was one evening when we were joined by some American friends of his for drinks in the bar before curtain up.

"I don't remember their names except for one man who was called Boris. He and his wife had just spent a couple of months in the South of France and he was very tanned and looked incredibly handsome in a white suit. We went into the theatre and I was sitting between Boris and the theatre critic. Just then four other friends of his arrived and sat in the row in front of us. One of them turned round and said, "Good evening, Mr Karloff." The penny dropped – I was sitting next to Boris Karloff whose movies had scared me senseless throughout my childhood. Even if I didn't have a good memory, I am sure I would have remembered that forever!

"I was on such a roll during those wild years. It was like being on a treadmill and finding it couldn't stop. However, as time rolled by, it began to dawn that it was a rather vacuous life, and my stop-the-world-I-want-to-get-off moments became increasingly frequent.

"Just then a change of direction presented itself, in fact two possibilities were thrust at me within the space of a month and both, coincidentally, sprang from when I lived in Paris. The first time I was there I met a Hungarian mathematician who worked at the Sorbonne. We used to breakfast at the same *boulangerie* and often chatted. When I went back to Paris, after we two had parted, I bumped into him in the street. I knew that his hobby was sculpture and he invited me to his studio flat to have a look at some of his work. In the midst of appreciating some of his beautiful sculptures, I burst into tears, which took us both by surprise. I found myself telling him about my broken heart. We bonded that day and became good friends. Later the friendship developed in the way these things often do.

"Then, just as I was leaving Paris, he heard that he had got the job he applied for at the University of Montreal. Apart from the occasional card, I didn't hear any more from him until a long letter arrived. He wrote that the job was going well, he had found a charming apartment and please, please would I consider marrying him? He would send my fare and we could get married as soon as I arrived in Canada.

"I decided to delay my reply and give it some thought.

"Then equally unexpected, I received a letter from Paris. Do you remember I told you about an American I met? Well, he was not suggesting marriage, indeed he told me previously that his estranged French wife would never agree to a divorce. His question was would I think about returning to Paris to live with him? Decisions, decisions.

"In the end I said NO times two.

"And now I think it's time to sign off."

"I do so enjoy our conversations, Marge. Goodnight my love – until tomorrow."

One day, I told Odd about a vivid dream I had had the night before: we were travelling together on a train and the picture was of us in our twenties, talking and laughing. Then the train entered a tunnel, Odd came and sat next to me and we kissed, the longest and most loving kiss which ended as we came out of the tunnel but by then we were the ages we are now.

"What do you make of that?" I asked him.

"It might make a good ending for our story," he suggested and this led us into discussing the book. Do we have a message to pass on? Yes indeed, several, we agreed. Never give up. Life is precious. It is never too late to find love (or rekindle it, as we had done). "And," Odd added, "physical expressions of love need never stop."

"Agreed," I said. "I remember a conversation I once had with a patient of Tom's. She had a lavender-and-lace gentility about her. Her husband was quite a famous musician. They were both well into their eighties, and she confided in me one day with the unforgettable words, 'He is still my lover, you know.' I was about 38 at the time and I thought this was so sweet and quite extraordinary. Now I'm a member of the eighties club, I don't find it the least bit extraordinary, just normal and beautiful. Age is irrelevant, it's about attitude of mind. In one's youth one thinks the joy of sex is reserved exclusively for the young. You don't *really* know what it's like to be 'old' until you are. I could never imagine my parents making love, let alone my grandparents! My God, how laughable, no way…"

"You are right, Marge, it is about mindset. I have met people in their forties who are already 'old'. But you, my lovely girl, are an inspiration to everyone. However long you live, I cannot imagine that you will ever be too old for anything!"

"You're the same, Odd. Your spirit is young, your mind active and your creativity vivid and, AND you are as sexy and romantic now as you were in your twenties."

"Am I really, Marge? But my body is letting me down. Perhaps I have not paid enough attention to my health over the years."

"One's sell-by date is not set in stone," I said. "When one thinks about 'age', there are so many absurdities, especially in the West. For example, you could take 10 people from different backgrounds, all in reasonably good health and all the same age according to their birth certificates – let's say 70. Yet, in terms of their *real* age, by which I mean their participation in and enjoyment of life – what they put in and what they get out of it – they could all be different. However, according to all the man-made rules, we are put into age boxes throughout life: the age you are able to vote, take your driving test, consent to sex, buy alcohol, drink in a pub, see certain films and so on. Then at the other end of the scale, it's the age of retirement, the age of entitlement for the state pension, a free bus pass, free television licence, the age you are able to buy a Senior Railcard, or enjoy age-related discounts in certain shops … need I go on? Things may be organised differently in Norway but I'm sure you'll get my drift. Of course, society must have rules, the alternative is chaos. Nevertheless, I think we are rather age-obsessed. To be fair, there is increasing recognition of what I'm banging on about – 60 is the new 50 and so on. It is constantly being talked about. I think in one's golden years, one must be mindful that the mind is like an umbrella in the rain: it functions best when open. It is so important not to get into a rut. From time to time, I wake up in the morning and decide to do everything differently that day. For example, I'll have my bath before, instead of after, breakfast, I'll wear something I haven't worn for a year or so, walk to the shops instead of taking the bus, buy brands new to me and some unusual vegetables, try a new recipe, ring a friend as promised on my Xmas card … and so on. All small things perhaps, but it's very stimulating."

"So what exactly are you trying to say, Marge?"

"I'm not sure, darling. I just felt like pontificating!"

"Well, let's return to the message of our book. We hope it will help others by hearing about what we have experienced. You sum it up, Marge."

"Let's see. I would say, "Take heart dear octogenarians" – no, let's cast the net wider – "Take heart all who have reached the autumn of life. With the right mindset, there are no limits to what life has to offer. Of course, you must look after your health – that's axiomatic – but that to one side, be mindful of the following:

Don't get stuck in your ways

Try to live creatively

Never lose your spirit of adventure

Never stop learning

And never stop loving

When heads and hearts are young, age counts for nothing."

Chapter 18

Odd rang to tell me they had moved him, yet again. This time to another building called Øya Helsehus. He seemed pleased with his room and said they had provided him with a desk for his writing as well as all the usual comforts. The staff were attentive and he had settled in well. He told me he was going to try and write something for our book.

During our next telephone conversation, Odd said, "This – you and me thing – it's developing, isn't it?"

"I guess one could say that," I replied. Silently, I pondered, perhaps there is some truth in the saying, 'all things come to those who wait' – but half a century, that's a very long time!

As our conversation came to an end that day, he said, "Are you mine, Marge – are you mine?"

"I think you know the answer to that."

A few days later, I received a letter from him with the material for our book.

December 7ʰ 2010

My dear Marge

I just finished the telephone chat with you and now I will try to write a bit, although the form is far from Olympic. The best thing to do in my situation is to try to write, and concentrate on things I love – which points to you of course.

So, now, my contribution to our/your manuscript. Here we go.

I start with the moment when I received the famous telephone call from you. I must write it in English although it would have been better changing between Norwegian and English.

The Telephone

It was five o'clock and still I sat by the kitchen window. It felt as if I had been sitting there for weeks. This monotony for a long-time patient. How much can I tolerate? I looked out of the window. March – winter. The garden, grey in grey, God, how I needed colours.

Then, like a shot, the telephone rang. Who could it be? Someone trying to sell me something probably.

No, this was different. It was a female voice. It said some unusual things too. I hesitated. She spoke English, beautiful English. I really woke up. 'Are you around 80 years old, and is your name Odd?' I didn't answer at once, as I normally do, but wondered. It struck me that there was something well-known in the voice, something from far away, something with humour – could it be? I checked my intuition. It could be impressive sometimes.

I raised my voice and said as the well-trained teacher I thought I was.

'Yes – and my name is Odd – and who are you?'

The answer came quickly, 'It's Marge.' Pause – I made it long. This had to be digested. This must not be destroyed. Marge – I knew at once who it was, that voice, that tone, that special laughter. It had to be *my* Marge. Yes, it was my Marge from about 60 years ago. Such an incredibly long, long time, but yet so near, and very far from forgotten.

All of a sudden I exclaimed in a new engaged voice, 'You are really my Marge? Is it true? Is it you? What has happened?'

A river of laughter followed, oh God, how she enjoyed the situation.

'Yes, I am Marge.' I had to interrupt and I panted, 'Where on earth are you? Tell me.'

'I am off the coast of Norway.' She was clearly enjoying her air of mystery.

'What are you doing there?' I thought to myself, no fisheries at this time and it is definitely not the swimming season.

'I am on a cruise,' she said. Norway is a long country but not caring about the geographical details, I asked, 'How did you find me, Marge?'

'I found you in Narvik, the place where you were born.'

Well, that is the preliminary end of my contribution to the manuscript.

Now to other things –

Yesterday, Øya Helsehus, was hit by an epidemic of vomiting and diarrhoea – and the house was isolated. We were all shut in our rooms. Although I have not been hit like some of the others, I am in rather bad form. Nevertheless, I availed myself of the opportunity to write the start of my contribution. Later, Arne Jørgen will collect this letter and some more translated poems for posting to you.

Just now I was given permission to go to the balcony for a cigarette! It tasted so good, my dear.

Otherwise this is like a prison. Without my long training previously in isolation, I would have been in a horrible state, disease plus forced isolation.

I hope my bits and pieces for our story will be useful for you.

I enclose a warm hug to my lovely girl. Remember, I miss you. I miss you a lot.

Yours, Odd

It was interesting to read our two accounts, side by side and the thoughts each of us had during that unforgettable telephone conversation. My journey to the Arctic turned out to be a journey of the heart – with all its bittersweet layers. So I didn't see the Aurora Borealis in all its glorious colours, as I had hoped, but instead I had found something of far greater beauty.

Odd must have been reviewing his life because in our next telephone conversation, he said, "It wouldn't have worked before, would it?"

"That is the third time you have posed that question over the past year, and my answer is still the same – possibly not, but we'll never know."

I knew he wanted me to agree with him unreservedly – but how could I? The jury was still out as far as I was concerned, and would remain so. Was he trying to convince me – or himself – or was it still the guilty conscience he was trying to ease?

Anyway, WHAT wouldn't have worked? That was *my* question. Our personalities were in harmony, our sense of values, likes and dislikes were so similar, as was the way we looked at life, the way we could make every moment we spent together so alive. And our sublime lovemaking was off the charts – so what exactly wouldn't have worked?

My mind wandered back to a letter I had received from him just prior to leaving Australia in 1953. He had asked me what my views were on marriage and I told him. In reply to my letter he said:

With great interest I have read your views on marriage. Of course it is an advantage in love with contrasts. But what is love alone without common interests? Old people keep telling me that nothing is more writing-in-the-sand than the promise of love. Love is a flower that always fades away and when the autumn comes there must be a substitute, and that is the sameness of plans and interests. That is what people tell me. I do not know.

I think it must be dreadful to sacrifice love for a sort of sober connection between two people. A sort of matter-of-fact marriage where the woman is the most suitable person to bear your children, to answer your questions at the dinner table etc. I believe it is a matter of inheritance, of milieu, of experience. If you are brought up in a home where love exists, you believe in it. You believe that love can give your life the beauty that is the necessity to live on.

I wondered who the 'old people' were who had talked to him about these matters. His Mother perhaps? Or older relatives or friends? And had their words of wisdom stayed with him?

Of course with hindsight, I concede there were certain practical issues, such as climate, language, way of life etc, to be considered.

It occurred to me that there was something else I hadn't thought of before. When we first met, I was on that world trip with my Mother. Did he perceive me as a spoilt little rich girl with not a serious thought in her head? If that *was* his first impression, I hope it changed with the passage of time.

I do recall one occasion when he was helping me on with my jacket – an obviously-expensive leather jacket – and he said, "Oh, my luxury girl, how could I ever provide you with such things?" and I retorted, "You wouldn't need to, there is much more to life than material possessions. If all I wanted was a life of plenty, I would return to Australia and live with my Mother, but that is not at all the way I see things." And Odd said, "So tell me your list of priorities."

"Top of my list – people, love, friendships. The acquisition of knowledge and, most importantly, putting it to good use. What Buddhists call 'Right Occupation'; Nature, of course, in all moods and guises, and creativity – music and the arts in all their manifestations."

And I remember he replied, "That is an admirable list, Marge."

I reminded myself that, during the course of my life, I had known both ends of the financial spectrum. There is no doubt that being free of money worries has much to recommend it, but wealth alone does not make you happy.

True happiness comes from within.

Enough of my musings. Was I *still* searching for the reasons that brought about his change of heart? Perhaps I needed validation that our love had been real in the 1950s and not just a product of my 20-something-year-old imagination.

Face the painful fact, I murmured to myself. In the end, he loved Sigrid more than me – and the added bonus was similar backgrounds and the sameness of interests and plans.

Suddenly, my sensible inner voice screamed, 'Shut the f … up! Stop overthinking. You experienced, in your twenties, the kind of love that most people never know, no matter how long they live. And, what's more,' my inner voice reminded me, 'it is happening all over again – so who's a lucky girl?!'

The phone rang, jolting me out of my dreamlike state. It was Odd.

"Why are you there, Marge – and I am here?"

"Separation always was our problem, wasn't it? That tormenting distance that constantly dogged our relationship – and history seems to be repeating itself, as it often does – but if you need me, I will come to Trondheim, whatever the weather and stay and stay."

"It is such a dreadful winter here now, I think we must be patient and wait until we can share the Spanish sunshine together. On the other hand, there is so much I want to tell you, and discuss with you."

He then told me that Marie had sent him a poem by DH Lawrence, which he read to me. Clearly, Odd's thoughts were turning again towards death. He said he had rung an old friend of his, a priest, who had promised to visit him.

"Marge, write me a letter about death. I want to know your thoughts and beliefs."

Facing life-threatening illness, of course, forces one to come to terms with one's own mortality. Odd had already done this so eloquently in his poetry. But then there had been some degree of remission, a plateau had been reached which allowed us to spend many wonderful weeks together, and the possibility of death never intruded on our thoughts. Indeed, we had planned ahead quite a bit – Spain in February, Cyprus in March, then back to my house in Kent for the spring. With luck, perhaps we would even manage that holiday in Italy that had been talked about so many moons ago.

Now, however, I was beginning to wonder whether we would even be fortunate enough to meet in Spain, let alone anywhere else.

Boxley, December 19th 2010
My very dear Odd

I have read the DH Lawrence poem many times now. It is so moving – and deeply thought-provoking. In fact it has triggered, in me, a new train of thought – and many complex feelings! I can readily understand your reactions.

I sit here in the warmth and comfort of The Old House with everything I need – except my Odd – so, no shoulder to rest my head on, no hands to hold … And then I think of you living that strange parallel existence in the Helsehus.

I try to imagine what it must be like: the monotony, the frustration of no longer being in control of your life, the uncertainties, the physical problems, the mental anguish – my heart weeps – but you never complain. I do so admire your courage, Odd.

Some weeks ago I thought long and hard about what your Marge, your distant Marge, might be able to do to help your situation in some small way. I decided to focus on promoting your beautiful poetry which richly deserves the widest possible audience. With some help from your new friends, who have also taken you to their hearts, we are making good progress! As soon as this Arctic weather becomes more reasonable, I plan to go to London to pursue the other contacts I have made. I want so much to help in any way I can. Of course I cannot share your physical problems, but perhaps we should be sharing – in much greater depth – thoughts, feelings, concerns…

It is quite a long time now since you were given 'the bad news'. Initially, I am sure you went through various stages and these too I try to imagine. Perhaps denial comes first, then disbelief, a touch of 'why me', followed maybe by anger and depression until, finally, one capitulates, and acceptance of the situation is achieved.

I have been thinking of various things I have said to you in recent weeks – 'never give up', 'you have so much to live for', 'we want – need even – more time together', 'hold on very tightly', 'the power of positive thought', etc, etc. My God, how I have babbled on! Most probably you are fed up with all the platitudes. Please forgive me if that is the case.

In discussing the DHL poem, I realised that what is of paramount importance is your desire for peace. I know you have expressed a lot in your poems about facing death, dying, reviewing your life – but perhaps that process is not yet complete and there is more you really need to talk about.

In the West, we are not much good at talking about death, it is not our custom and yet to do so can be very liberating if done with total freedom. A bit like solving a problem before the problem presents itself!

We octogenarians should express our emotions about dying. I believe we need to face our fears. Fear, after all, is human and universal. For myself, I suppose my greatest fear would be to develop dementia, become totally dependent, and take many years to slowly disintegrate mentally and physically (which of course is the result of my experience). However, just in case, I have tried to provide a solution with my Living Will. I think I told you about that. I fear as well prolonged physical pain – and goodness knows how many other fears I have tucked away, all of which require scrutiny! When one's time here on earth is running short, I think it is important to identify one's own deepest truth. We need to recognise our own spirituality and get in touch with our own inner strength.

Once we become members of the Over Eighties Club, we are *all* facing death, it is just a question of timing. I am deeply grateful for my health and abundant energy so far – but one's mortality is like a game of roulette. Death is unpredictable. Only yesterday one of Boxley's residents died very suddenly at 70-something – an aneurysm, I believe. A wonderfully-fast way to make one's exit, like turning off a light. So, who knows, I might go first. Whichever way round it is, I hope I can be with you at the end. How one makes one's departure from this life is very important, or so I believe.

I fear this letter is becoming a touch melancholic! It is meant to be helpful of course, but I am not at all sure I am succeeding!

I love our daily phone calls but would much rather be with you to hold hands, and look into your eyes so that we could *really* communicate. I know I have said it before, but it is worth repeating – you can say anything at all to me, there are no restrictions – thoughts, fears, feelings of guilt or anger, regrets – whatever you need to explore. I am here for you Odd with a heart full of unconditional love and understanding.

We have so many layers to us haven't we, just like an onion, and some of our emotions are bound to be repressed. I do believe that when we reach this stage of life we need to dig deeply in order to resolve any troubled thoughts and anxieties, including dealing with practical matters that need attention – and, whilst there is still time, things that need to be said to whoever should be said. I am sure all this is essential in order to reach that state we call Peace.

I am so glad you are back in my life Odd Irtun!

Ever

Your Marge

Christmas was fast approaching. Odd was invited by his dear friend of over 40 years, Håkon Bleken, to spend Christmas Eve with them. Patients who could manage it were encouraged to go out for such occasions. For myself, plans were in hand to spend Christmas Day with 10 local friends, cooking and enjoying our Christmas feast together.

Chapter 19

I wondered what 2011 would have in store. I reminded myself that just as I used to keep every single memento from the 1950s, now in 2010/11, I remembered every single loving sentence Odd uttered. I was grateful for my good memory but actually this was different. It was as if his words were engraved in my heart.

Our telephone conversations and letters continued. I was concerned that he seemed to be eating less and less, and the things he told me he did eat seemed so inappropriate. I pointed out that it was one thing to be dying of stomach cancer, but quite another to be dying of starvation. I could not understand why they had not put him on a special diet. He could no longer cope with any solid food, so why wasn't he being given nutritious soups, liquidised vegetables and proteins, perhaps porridge. He listened very carefully and asked if I would send some recipes etc, which he would get one of his friends to make and take into him. I did as requested but am not sure whether this ever happened.

It was clear that he was getting weaker and one day the call came that I had been dreading. "Marge, I promised I would not hold anything back from you, so I feel I should tell you that I am now firmly in the grip of this disease. I think the end is getting nearer and I would like you to help me plan my funeral."

This was all said in a very matter of fact voice, which I knew he was doing to help me. I responded in the same tone, even though I felt my heart was breaking. He had already chosen the church and had written out full instructions, every detail.

"There won't be a dry eye in the house," he said impishly. He wanted me to help him choose the music. We discussed various possibilities. He liked the Negro Spiritual, 'Sometimes I feel like a motherless child', which he said he would arrange to have played on the trombone, also one or two songs, he knew some soloists – and Grieg, of course.

"And don't forget our special music," I said.

"Indeed, 'Secret Garden'. Did you notice I used that as background music for the DVD?"

It felt as if we were organising some concert or other – but it wasn't, it was his funeral we were discussing.

"Marge, my dear, it is not about to happen any minute, I promise. It's just that I want to get it organised whilst I'm still able to do so."

A couple of days later, I rang Odd's friend, Roger, who was a frequent visitor. I wanted to hear how things were from someone else. Roger told me that on his visit to the hospital that day, Odd was refusing to see any visitors.

"I am going to book a flight right away," I said.

"What if he won't see you?"

"Oh, he will. I know he will."

I was able to get on a flight the following day and I also rang the Radisson Blu Hotel, where we had stayed the previous summer. Strangely, the room they gave me was right next door to the one we had stayed in. I dumped my suitcase and went straight to the hospital to which Odd had been moved from the Helsehus.

"You are full of surprises, Marge. It seems only a few hours since I was speaking to you on the other side of the North Sea – and now here you are! I am so glad you came. It must be love," he grinned.

"Something like that," I replied with a smile. I sat by his bed as close to him as I could get. We held hands – and just looked at each other for the longest time. Verbal communication was unnecessary, we were so attuned to each other. At long last, Odd broke the silence and said, "I love that colour on you."

"You mean my scarf? Shocking pink, it's called."

"You know, Marge, you are a beautiful old woman."

"Thank you … I think!"

"That didn't come out quite the way I intended. Actually, you have such a young face for…"

"Let me guess … an old woman."

"I am trying to compliment you, Marge, but I'm not expressing myself very well, am I? Let me try again. I love your hair, your eyes, your mouth, your youthful way of being."

"Success, Odd, stop right there! That a very pretty compliment. Thank you. Anyway, I'm not old – it's just accumulated youth!"

We both laughed – and it was heart-warming to hear him laugh.

The grip of his hand in mine never lessened the whole time I was there – and yet it was obvious he was very weak. It was as if we were trying to hang on to life and love. The words at the end of one his recent letters came back to me – "No one must be allowed to take this away from us."

The following day, in spite of not sleeping much, he appeared to be in reasonably good spirits, although the pain and discomfort took over from time to time.

I was able to tell him I had heard that "In Focus" magazine, with his Cyprus poems, photographs and the biographical notes, was now published – but I had not yet seen a copy. He was delighted with this news.

I then asked Odd if the visit from his priest friend had been helpful. "Yes, indeed, in fact he came a couple of times which was very good of him because he is also old and not at all well. Did I tell you how much I appreciated your letter, Marge? It helped a lot. I think it is important to be able to discuss death with someone close to you. There is something I must tell you. Marie will be arriving here within the next couple of days – and she too wants to be with me at the end."

"That's fine, Odd." I joked, "You have two hands, so we can hold one each."

Odd laughed, "You are amazing, Marge." He was looking very tired so I suggested he should try and have some sleep whilst I went in search of a sandwich and a cup of coffee.

When I returned, he asked me if I would get into bed with him, he felt I was too far away sitting on a chair. "I want you in my arms," he said. God knows I wanted that too but it just wasn't practical. He was attached to so many pieces of equipment – and hospital beds are very narrow. So with regret, I declined his invitation, but it would have been amusing to see the medical staff's reactions.

Later that day, he told me he could not feel his legs and he asked me to massage them for him, which I did. Since my last visit, he had lost much more weight – I had to fight back the tears.

"When you return home, Marge, you are going to say to yourself – well that was a rather expensive trip – for nothing."

"Odd," I protested, "this is not nothing!" Being together, no matter what the circumstances, could never be considered as 'nothing'.

"You are right, as ever, my wise and wonderful girl. Tell me, how is our book progressing?"

"Slowly but surely it is taking shape. Writing it, I must say, is quite cathartic. There have been days when I've felt as if I was in therapy. Quite often I feel as though we were writing it together. I see your eyes, hear your voice and feel your presence."

"I do hope, Marge, that those feelings will continue until the last chapter."

When I arrived at the hospital the next morning, there was a big change in him. There had been alarming deterioration during the night and he appeared to be heavily sedated. I felt that his time on this earth was rushing by like an avalanche down a mountain – and just as unstoppable. All I could do was sit by the bed and hold his hand. Some three hours later, he stirred, opened his eyes and smiled at me weakly, but as warmly as ever. It felt as if he had been right to the edge and come back again. He wanted something to drink. No sooner had it gone down than it came up again.

The distressing vomiting continued on and off all day. I took on the mantle of nurse as they seemed to be short-staffed and he needed constant care and attention. "This is so unpleasant for you, Marge, my dear."

"Nothing about you could ever be unpleasant – please don't worry about it, I'm fine." When he became a little more settled, he said, "It is so difficult letting go of the things you love." He squeezed my hand. "No more music, art, literature, the beauty of Nature, all one's wonderful friends. I wonder what will happen to all my papers, paintings, books, audio-visual materials…" his voice trailed off. He was in and out of consciousness all day.

I could tell from his eyes that he had found peace – and later, when I posed the question, he assured me he had. He was calm, there was no sense of fear and when he was conscious he was utterly present, totally in the moment.

I had to accept that he was going now at breakneck speed towards the end of his life. It was so heartbreaking and, at the same time, so moving to watch his life gradually slipping away. I could do nothing but hold his hand and silently offer my heart to this special human being with such a beautiful mind and soul – always interesting, amusing, sensitive and tender. This man whose love I had been privileged to know not once, but twice in my lifetime. And now he was leaving me – AGAIN – and I could do nothing to stop it, just as before.

I bent over and kissed him very lightly on the forehead. I wasn't sure whether he was conscious or not. "*Jeg elsker deg,* Odd Fredrik Irtun," I whispered. "*Jeg elsker deg.*" I saw a slight movement of awareness and the faintest hint of a smile.

When I got back to the hotel, it was about 10:00 p.m., but I couldn't bear the thought of food. I went to the bar instead and had a large G&T. The waitress remembered me/us from our stay there last summer. It was quite a relief to just chat to someone about nothing in particular.

When I went upstairs to my room, I suddenly felt hot and shivery and I was experiencing all sorts of strange symptoms – sickness, headache, dizziness, inability to urinate. What was going on? Was I coming down with flu or had I picked up some bug or other, perhaps at the hospital? Of course, it had been a long and emotionally exhausting day. Watching my Odd come face to face with his own dying had been an overwhelmingly poignant and powerful experience.

I didn't sleep a wink all night and, by 6:00 a.m., I decided the best course of action would be to try and get a flight home as soon as possible. Feeling so unwell, I couldn't visit Odd and there was no point in being sick, on my own, in a hotel.

There was no point either in asking for a doctor as I knew it was nothing serious, I just needed to go home, be on my own and cry. The airline was able to book me on a flight for that afternoon although I had to go via Oslo and change planes. No matter.

I knew this was the best thing to do but I did feel as if I was deserting him before the end – and I had so wanted to be with him until his very last breath. On the other hand, Marie was due to arrive and probably his daughter was coming down from the North as well, so one way and another...

I tried ringing him several times but his mobile was switched off so I decided to write to him instead.

Radisson Blu, February 11th 2011
My dearest Odd

I have just booked a flight home for this afternoon, but I didn't dare come to the hospital this morning as I seem to have developed a heavy cold overnight and I don't want to give you any of my bugs, you have enough of your own to cope with. In any event, I hate goodbyes – and I am not sure I could deal with this particular one.

Letting go is so difficult isn't it – and yet I know clinging to anything or anyone is definitely not wise either. Of course, I will shed tears – buckets of them – but I shall try hard to think of your dying process as merely an extension of your life.

"Tomorrow or the next life – which comes first, we never know."

Is there a next life? Is there reincarnation? Is there this? Is there that? How long have we all wrestled with the unanswerable questions. I remain convinced, however, that there is something – our innermost essence – that is indestructible. Buddhists talk about the essential Nature of Mind as being absolutely and always untouched by death. Of course, every religion has its Fundamental Truth, it's just that it gets a variety of interpretations and names. Christians call it God, Buddhists call it Buddha Nature, Hindus call it the Self – and so on. If I try to think in really simple terms, then what survives death is Love and Goodness which, my dear one, you have in abundance.

I have always tried to turn negatives into positives, so how do I look at the events of these past 11 months? Above all with gratitude. I am so glad our paths crossed again. Rediscovering each other has been AMAZING – the weeks we have spent together, the letters, the daily telephone calls. How I shall miss it all. Trembling together in the music, our discussions, the humour and playfulness – it was all so natural, open, undemanding and meaningful.

Thank you for being you, Odd – and thank you for your tenderness and love.

Always and Forever

Your Marge

Chapter 20

The journey home was a long one, which gave me plenty of time to think. As the plane started taxiing along the runway I began to relax. About 20 minutes into the flight, I realised that all my symptoms had gone. This was a light bulb moment. I admit to being just a touch psychosomatic – and sensitive to boot. Why hadn't I realised what was going on? The past three days I had spent with Odd had been so intense. We had held hands throughout and, of course, I had 'picked up' his distressing symptoms. Something deep inside me wanted to share in his suffering. The power of the mind is extraordinary!

I kept wanting to cry but didn't want to make an ass of myself on the plane, so I just sank into a dreamlike state and let the thoughts come and go. I remembered my Robert's process of dying. For the last months of his life, he was in a Home because I had finally collapsed under the strain of nursing him. During his final two weeks, they gave me a room next to his so that I could be with him all the time – and at the end. In spite of his advanced dementia, I had witnessed a huge transformation in him. There was no doubt that he too had found Peace. I firmly believe that the way we die is of importance and I remember doing everything possible to make the atmosphere in his room calm and reassuring, especially during his last day. I played a tape of Gregorian chants, which I knew he loved, dimmed the lights and lit lots of candles and incense. Then I held him until his life ebbed away.

"A lifetime is like a flash of lightning in the sky." Buddhist teachings kept running through my head. They had helped me throughout my life and I needed that help now. The truth of impermanence, perhaps the only thing we can hold onto. Everything that is born will die. All we have is the NOW. The importance of acknowledging and accepting the fundamental connection between life and death. The Buddha said, "This existence of ours is as transient as autumn clouds."

Memories of Odd and all our special moments, of course, dominated my thoughts on the flight. What a presence he had, and such a warm, immediate personality. He could charm the birds out of the trees. He had it all in his twenties – and still had it in his eighties!

Snatches from his letters, bits I knew by heart, kept running through my mind – some from way back, like: "What matters is that we love each other – beyond time and distance", "I suppose we are able to stand anything as long as we *know* that we belong to each other", "What does it matter if we are separated – when we KNOW that we are one", and, from a fairly recent letter written in hospital, "There is so much that has not been said during all this time we were not together. When will I be able to say all that ought to be said to you, all you deserve to hear."

Unfortunately, Odd never came out of hospital and so our various travel plans were never realised. When I visited him in February, he was too ill – so the things he wanted to express must be left to the creative faculty of my mind.

Not in my wildest imagination would I have ever thought it possible to meet Odd again. And not only did we meet, but we found love all over again. At 80, for God's sake! Perhaps a piece of my heart had always been his, but I had to get on with my life, and so all those feelings were wrapped-up with his letters in that heavily-Sellotaped parcel. I suppose it was not exactly surprising to discover that my feelings for him were immutable.

Sitting across the aisle from me was a couple in their early twenties, totally lost in each other. I thought to myself, young love is so sweet – and then I chuckled, come to think of it, there is nothing wrong with old love either!

My next reflection was that, at this very moment, there must be countless thousands around the world in their dying days, and the loved ones they leave behind to suffer are all weeping and trying to make sense of it. This, I said to myself, is but a microcosm of the macrocosm.

By the time I got home from the airport, it was too late to ring Odd. However, there were three messages from him on my answering service. Obviously, he thought he was ringing me at the hotel when, in fact, he was ringing me in the UK. I guess his confusion was due to all the medication. His first message was 10:00 a.m. that morning. He said, "I'm waiting for you but don't rush. I seem to be sleeping a lot which is no fun for you. So no hurry."

In the next message, he said, "This is another really bad day. It's such a strain for both of us. There are so many unpleasant things today, as well. At the moment, I am waiting to be given a catheter."

The third message was early evening. He said, "I want to hear your reaction to my previous calls. Please, please ring me." There was a pause and then he said, with such feeling, "I love you, Marge." I cried and cried.

As it turned out, these were his last words to me. My messaging service keeps calls for three weeks and I played those messages from Odd over and over again. It was so good to be able to hear his voice, especially the final words.

The following morning, I rang his mobile but all I heard was a sort of grunt. I guessed he was barely conscious but I spoke nonetheless, explaining that I had left because I hadn't felt well but that I had written to him. It sounded as if he said, very faintly, something like, "No need" – but the words were blurred and barely audible. Then the line went dead. I have no idea whether he ever received my last letter to him.

Over the next few days, I telephoned continuously but each time it was either switched off or, if it rang, it was immediately disconnected. Fortunately, some of Odd's friends kindly kept me informed. It was clear that his body was gradually shutting down.

Early on the morning of February 20th 2011, I received a call from Roger telling me Odd had died that morning at 6.30 a.m. He promised to let me know when the funeral would be, as he knew that I wanted to be there.

It took place on February 25th. Roger could not have been more supportive. He collected me from my hotel and, as we drove to Vår Frue Kirke, he said he could still hear Odd's voice, whenever he spoke about me, saying, "Gosh, what a woman!"

It was a beautiful church, the same one in which he once gave a poetry reading. When I walked in and saw his photograph lit by a candle and then, at the far end of the church, the white coffin surrounded by flowers, I really didn't know how I was going to keep myself together. The church was full, and so many people I hadn't met before came up and said, "You must be Marge."

Of course, Marie was there. We managed to overcome any feelings of awkwardness. Odd had always told me she was a very generous person and I had a fine example of her generous spirit some months later when we spoke on the telephone. She told me that in Odd's dying moments, he called out my name and she felt sure I would like to know that he was thinking of me until the end.

I also met Odd's daughter. I could not see any resemblance at all on any level, which was interesting. Someone at the funeral told me Odd had written a poem about meeting me again – but he never told me about it. Perhaps he considered it was still work in progress. Then Odd's friend, Barbro, told me he had confided in her that it was Marge he wanted to be with.

When I looked at the printed order of service, I was disappointed that there was no mention of "Secret Garden". All the other music we had discussed was there and beautifully played and sung. There were eulogies, of course, which I couldn't really understand but I could feel the huge affection that everyone was showing for Odd – my first love and my last love.

Then something quite wonderful happened. Just as everyone was beginning to file out of the church, the music from "Secret Garden" was played.

Of course, he hadn't forgotten. This was so typical of him. It was his beautifully subtle way of sending me a very personal farewell and a secret message of love.

ACKNOWLEDGEMENTS

My thanks to Martin Hosmer for suggesting that his son-in-law, Richard Maskell, might be persuaded to read my draft manuscript. Richard, who has been in publishing for most of his life, agreed – although he didn't even know me at the time. He found it to be a 'wonderful story, uplifting and thought-provoking' and offered his help. Richard has steered and counselled me throughout the process and, with the help of his colleague Matt Drew, designed the book and even converted it into an ebook. So, a very big thank you!

I am grateful also to my stepson, Nick, for designing my website – and for his unfailing enthusiasm.

My thanks too to those friends who gave me support and encouragement along the way – in particular Tricia, Clare, Anna, Linda and Hazel, not forgetting Arne Jorgern in Norway.

Finally, and most importantly, my thanks to Odd whose idea it was that I should write our story. 'Tell it exactly the way it happened,' he said. 'No need to embellish, no need to conceal – and of course you have my permission to quote all my letters.'

I am glad I have been able to fulfil his dying wish. Thank you Odd for being such an important part of my life.

Also by Margery Bloomfield

TREE OF LIFE

A history of the European School of Osteopathy –
and much more…

A personal story full of anecdotes and reminiscences in which the
author recalls the changes, difficulties and success stories over the
School's first 50 years.

'It is a book that is a joy to read … a treasure trove of valuable
historical information on an important sector of the history of
osteopathy in Britain to which only Margery was privy, as well as
citing amusing anecdotes.'
OSTEOPATHY TODAY

'…an enthralling insider's view of a unique adventure and a
heart-warming story of what can be done, against all odds, if you
believe in your mission and work with faith and good heart.
I loved the book and could hardly put it down.'

'…told with affection and humour. It is a remarkable story of an
extraordinary woman – a valuable legacy for osteopathy students
both past and present, not to be missed.'
THE OSTEOPATH